대학영작문

영어문장의 이해와 활용

대학영작문

영어문장의 이해와 활용

김종실 저

형설출판사
www.hyungseul.co.kr

| 머리말 |

영어를 배우는 궁극적인 목표는 영어를 통한 원활한 의사소통일 것이다. 최근 영어교육 전문가들이나 각종 미디어는 한국어 화자들이 정확한 영어문장을 구사해야 한다는 강박관념에 얽매여서 문장 구사에 두려움을 갖거나 소극적이다 보니 영어로 의사소통 하는 데 있어서 어려움을 겪고 있다고 지적하고 있다. 즉 문법적인 문장을 만드는 데 급급할 것이 아니라 다소 비문법적인 표현을 쓰더라도 되도록 자신감을 갖고 과감하게 대화를 이어가며 의미를 전달하는 데 중점을 두는 것이 좋다고 판단하는 추세이다.

그렇다면 말이 아닌 글로써 의사소통하는 경우에는 상황이 어떠할까? 작문의 경우에는 이야기가 상당히 달라진다. 말로 하는 언어 구사와 글로 써서 기록하는 언어 구사 사이에는 차이가 있다. 즉 순간적이고 일시적인 성격을 갖는 발화와 달리 비교적 시간의 제한에 구애받지 않으며 영구적으로 기록될 수 있는 작문의 경우에는 사실상 문장의 정확성이 중요한 요소가 될 수밖에 없다. 더군다나 영어권 국가들을 포함하는 서구사회는 기록을 중요시하는 문화를 발전시켜 왔으며 기록을 통한 의사소통에 있어서 정확성과 형식을 중요시한다. 즉 영어 작문은 기본적으로 정확한 영어 문장의 구사 능력을 필요로 하고 더 나아가 단락과 에세이, 리포트나 논문 등 확장된 영역에서의 간결하고 논리적인 내용을 필요로 한다. 따라서 외국어인 영어를 매개체로 작문을 통해서 의사소통하는 일은 상당히 부담스럽고 어려운 작업일 수 있고 그런 점에서 사실상 작문은 영어학습자들에게 궁극적으로 가장 어려우며 종종 기피하는 영역이기도 하다.

그렇다면 영어 문장을 정확하게 구사하기 위해서는 어떤 점에 중점을 두어야 할까? 학습자들에게는 영어가 생소한 문법적 규칙이나 제약을 가진 언어로 생각되겠지만 실제로 대다수의 한국어 화자들이 어려움을 겪는 또 다른 원인은 영어가 가진 다양하고 광범위한 어휘용례 때문이다. 역사적으로 프랑스어와 그 조상어인 라틴어 어휘가 대거 차용됨으로써 영어 어휘는 방대해졌고 본래 갖고 있던 어휘적 특성과 더불어 다양한 어휘군이 형성되고 각 어휘의 용례 또한 복잡하고 다양하게 되었다. 즉 영어문장을 잘 구사하려면 문법적 지식과 더불어 어휘마다 그 용례를 살피고 익히는 노력이 필요하다.

그런 점에서 이 책은 기본적인 영어문장을 구사하는 데 있어서 한국어 화자들이 반드시 알아야 할 필수적인 내용을 담고자 하였다. 즉 완벽한 문장을 구사할 수 있는 능력이 부족한 학생들을 대상으로 하며 문장을 정확하고 자연스럽게 구사할 수 있도록 학습하는 것을 돕는 데 그 목적이 있다. 그러한 목표를 달성하기 위해 책의 내용을 한국어 화자들이 영어 문장을 원활하게 구사하기 위해서 필수적으로 습득해야 하는 기초 영역과 한국어에 없거나 달라서 오류를 많이 보일 뿐만 아니라 기피하는 경향을 보이는 부분에 집중하고자 하였다.

이 책의 보다 구체적인 내용은 다음과 같다. 우선 기본적으로 한국어 화자들이 영어의 구조를 이해하고 문장을 구사하기 위해 반드시 학습해야 할 필수 영역이라고 판단되는 동사의 용례와 문장구조에 많은 부분을 할당하였다. 또한 영어문장 구사에 필수적인 동사시제를 이해하고 활용할 수 있도록 하였다. 더불어 다소 복잡한 개념을 표현하기 위해 필요한 복합절을 습득하고 활용하도록 하였으며, 명사와 명사를 수식하는 수식어구의 활용과 영어에서 다방면으로 자주 사용되는 전치사의 다양한 용례 등을 소개하고 학습을 통해 작문을 하는 데 활용할 수 있도록 유도하고자 하였다. 물론 책의 내용에 아직 부족한 부분이 많을 것으로 짐작되나 아무쪼록 학습자들이 확실한 신념과 자신감을 갖고 정확한 기본 영어 문장들을 구사하는 데 이 책이 조금이나마 도움을 줄 수 있기를 바란다.

2016년

김종실

| 목차 |

Grammar Tips

문법용어

Adjective: 형용사

Adjectival Phrase: 형용사구

Adverb: 부사

Adverbial Phrase: 부사구

Complement: 보어, 보충어

- Object Complement: 목적보어
- Subject Complement: 주격보어

Determiner: 한정사

- Article: 관사
- Demonstrative: 지시사

Gerund: 동명사

Infinitive: 부정사

- to-infinitive: to-부정사
- ø-infinitive: 원형부정사

Interrogative: 의문사

Noun: 명사

- Countable Noun: 가산명사
- Uncountable Noun: 불가산명사

Object: 목적어

- Direct Object: 직접목적어
- Indirect Object: 간접목적어

Particle: 불변화사

Phrasal Verb: 구동사

Preposition: 전치사

Pronoun: 대명사

  Possessive: 소유대명사

Sentential Adverb: 문장부사

Subject: 주어

Subjunctive: 가정법

Verb: 동사

  Auxiliary Verb: 조동사

  Main Verb: 본동사

wh-pronoun: 의문대명사

I

동사용례에 따른 문장구조의 이해 및 연습

I 동사용례에 따른 문장구조의 이해 및 연습

A. 동사용례에 따른 문장의 구조

영어문장(sentence)은 주부(주어, subject)와 술부(predicate)로 구성되어 있으며 문장의 주부는 명사구, 그리고 술부는 동사구 등의 구(phrase)로 구성되어 있다. 다시 말해서 기본적으로 영어문장을 구성하기 위해서는 주어 명사와 시제가 표시된 동사가 있어야 한다. 이 때 각 동사의 특징에 따라 문장은 복잡해질 수도 있고 간단할 수도 있다. 아래에서 보듯이 영어 문장들은 동사의 성격에 따라 다양한 문장구조를 형성하며 한 동사가 여러 가지 구문을 구성하기도 한다.

(1) He came yesterday.

(2) She put the book on the table.

(3a) The boys looked happy.

(3b) When I look at you, I see forgiveness.

(4a) He was getting bored.

(4b) Generally I get to work at 9:30.

(4c) I want to get a job at New York.

(4d) Get him a large box.

(4e) I got him dressed up.

(1)번 문장에서 동사 'come'은 그 자체만으로 주어 'He'와 함께 문장을 구성한다. 즉 보충적 요소가 필요하지 않다. 'yesterday'의 경우 시간을 나타

내는 부사어로 문장의 동사와는 연관이 없는 부가적 요소이다. (2)의 예에서 'put'의 경우 '책을 탁자에 놓다'라는 의미를 위해 보충어로 'the book'의 목적어(Object)와 'on the table'과 같은 장소를 나타내는 부사구가 필요하다. (3a)의 'look' 동사는 '보이다'라는 의미로 쓰여 'happy'와 같은 보어(주격보어: Subject Complement)가 필요하다. 그러나 자동사인 관계로 목적어가 오지 못하여 (3b)에서처럼 '…을 보다'의 의미로 쓰이기 위해서는 목적어를 갖는 전치사와 함께 쓰여 'look at' 자체가 타동사처럼 쓰이는 구동사(phrasal verb)를 구성한다. (4)의 'get' 동사의 경우 다양한 의미와 용례를 갖는 영어동사들 중 하나이다. (4a)에서처럼 'become'의 의미로 쓰이기도 하고, (4b)에서처럼 'arrive'의 의미로 쓰이기도 한다. (4c)에서는 일반적인 목적어를 갖는 타동사로 쓰이며 (4d)에서는 '…에게 …을 가져다주다'의 의미로 쓰여 간접목적어와 직접목적어를 다 사용하는 문장을 구성한다. 한편 (4e)에서 'get' 동사는 '…로 하여금 …하게 하다'의 사역의 의미로 쓰여 목적어(him)와 목적보어(dressed up)와 함께 문장을 구성하게 된다.

이처럼 영어 동사는 그 자체만으로 주어와 함께 문장을 구성하기도 하고, 다른 보완적 요소들인 보충어(보어, 목적어, 부사어/Complement)와 더불어 다양한 문장을 구성한다. 즉 문장구조는 동사가 결정짓게 된다. 또한 위의 'get' 동사에서 보듯이 한 동사가 여러 의미로 쓰이거나 여러 다른 유형의 문장들을 구성하기도 한다. 따라서 영어문장을 제대로 구사하기 위해서는 동사가 실제 문장에서 어떻게 쓰이는지 동사의 용례를 반드시 알아야 한다.

본 장의 내용은 다음과 같이 구성되어 있다. 우선 학습자들이 기본적인 영어문장을 이해하고 구사하는 능력을 갖출 수 있도록 총 90개의 필수 영어 동사들의 구체적인 용례와 그 패턴이 제시되어 있다. 또한 학습자들이 이를 바탕으로 연습문제를 통하여 영어 동사의 다양한 문장구성을 활용하고 훈련하도록 되어 있다.

B. 동사의 용례에 근거한 문장의 이해 및 연습

1. accept

[1] accept + Noun(Direct Object) (+ Preposition…)

: 동사 accept 뒤에 목적어인 명사가 오는 경우이며 때로는 여러 의미의 전치사구(부사구)가 같이 쓰인다.

(1a) He accepted our invitation.

(1b) Everyone told me I should accept the job.

(1c) I never accept presents from clients.

(1d) I knew that they would accept my proposal.

(1e) All old clothes will be gratefully accepted by the organizers.

(1f) I've been accepted to graduate school.

(1g) Vietnam should be accepted back into the global economic community.

(1h) My daughter was accepted to Juilliard.

[2] accept + Noun + Preposition(as) + (being) Adjective/Noun

: 동사 accept 뒤에 목적어와 '…로서'의 의미로 as를 사용하는 전치사구가 오는 경우이며 이 때 관례상 전치사 'as' 뒤의 'being'이 생략되고 직접 형용사가 사용되기도 한다.

(2a) He never really accepted her as his own child.

(2b) He refused to accept his judgement as final.

(2c) They accept the risks as part of the job.

(2d) Most people would accept it as reasonable that an employer can protect its trade secrets.

[3] accept + Nominal Clause(Direct Object)

: 명사절이 목적어로 쓰이는 경우에 해당된다.

(3a) You would just have to accept what they told you.

(3b) He didn't accept that smoking causes bad health.

(3c) You just have to accept that we're never going to be rich.

[4] Other Usage

(4) He asked me to marry him and I accepted.

영작문제 :

a. 수표(*a check*)도 받으시나요? (수표도 되나요?)

b. 그는 지금 자신이 중년의 위기(*have a mid-life crisis*)를 맞고 있다는 사실을 인정할 수 없다.

c. 그들은 우리의 제안(*offer*)을 타당한 것(*valid*)으로 받아들였다.

2. call

[1] call + ø

: 뒤에 어떤 보충어(보어나 목적어) 없이 완전 자동사로 쓰인다.

(1a) May I ask who's calling?

(1b) David called when you were out.

[2] call + Preposition(for, to, etc.)…

: 종종 전치사와 함께 쓰이며 특히 '요구/요청하다'의 의미로 쓰일 때 'for'와 함께 쓰인다.

(2a) We called for help and they killed my son.

(2b) Mr Bush also called for a summit meeting of NATO countries in late June.

(2c) I just call to them and they come running down the field.

(2d) I called to him for help.

(2e) He called out to the man on the boat.

[3] call + Noun

: 일반 타동사로 목적어와 함께 쓰인다.

(3a) He called her son, but he did not hear her.

(3b) He called a meeting.

(3c) She called a taxi.

[4] call + Noun + Preposition…

: 동사 뒤에 목적어와 전치사구(부사구)가 오는 경우에 해당된다.

(4a) We called our friend by his nickname.

(4b) He had called him into his office on Tuesday.

[5] call + Noun(Indirect Object) + Noun(Direct Object)

: 간접목적어('…에게')와 직접목적어('…를')가 함께 오는 구문을 말한다.

(5a) We called him Jack, but his mother called him Jesse.

(5b) Olivia will be able to call you a cab as well as any doorman in Britain.

[6] call + Noun + to-infinitive/Adjective/Noun(Object Complement)

: 동사 뒤에 목적어와 목적어의 행위나 상태를 나타내는 목적보어가 오는 구문이다. 아래의 (6c)의 경우 위의 (5)번 용례에도 해당될 수 있다.

(6a) I call him fat.

(6b) He called us to help him.

(6c) I wouldn't call it a burden; I call it a responsibility

(6d) They called it foolish to turn away instructional help when the district has to lay off teachers.

영작문제 :

a. 그녀는 도움을 요청했다.

b. 이 꽃의 이름은 뭡니까? (이 꽃을 무엇으로 부릅니까?)

c. 그녀는 나를 게으르고(*lazy*) 이기적(*selfish*)이라고 했다.

3. decide

[1] decide + ø

(1a) Go on. You decide.

(1b) The public gets to decide.

(1c) Think about it very carefully before you decide.

[2] decide + Preposition…

: 동사 뒤에 전치사구(부사구)가 오는 구문으로써 다양한 의미의 전달을 위해 다양한 전치사가 쓰인다.

(2a) We have decided on selling our house.

(2b) It is difficult to decide between the two options.

(2c) I haven't decided about the book yet.

(2d) He decided against leaving.

(2e) The jury decided in favor of the defendant.

(2f) Martha could not decide about continuing or ending the marriage.

[3] decide + Noun

(3a) The goal that decided the match came just before the interval.

(3b) The case is to be decided by the court.

(3c) We understood he was letting us decide his fate.

(3d) He plans to hold a referendum to decide the issue once and for all.

[4] decide + (wh–pronoun +) to–infinitive

: 본동사(main verb) 이외의 주어의 행위와 관련된 서술이 필요할 경우 부정사(Infinitive) 즉 to–부정사(to–Infinitive)와 함께 쓰이며 의미상 의문사(wh–pronoun, 의문대명사)와 같이 쓰이기도 한다.

(4a) We decided to go to the movies.

(4b) He has decided to retire soon.

(4c) He couldn't decide what to do.

(4d) The young couple could not decide which house to buy.

(4e) I had a cold and couldn't decide whether to go to work or not.

[5] decide + Nominal Clause

: 의미상 필요할 경우 목적어 역할을 하는 명사절과 함께 쓰인다.

(5a) She decided that she would say no.

(5b) He decided that he would not smoke again.

(5c) It's entirely up to the victim to decide if they require help.

(5d) I decided that they were mistaken.

(5e) He decided (that) Franklin must be suffering from a bad cold.

[6] Other Usage

: (6a)의 'decide about'처럼 전치사와 함께 쓰여 구동사(phrasal verb)를 이룰 경우 구동사 전체가 타동사처럼 쓰여 목적어로 명사절을 갖기도 한다. 즉 결과적으로 전치사 뒤에 명사가 아닌 명사절이 오게 된다. (6b)~(6d)의 경우에는 decide가 목적어로 하여금 '…하게 하다, 하게끔 결정짓다'의 의미로 쓰이기도 한다.

(6a) It helped you to decide about whether you were going to tell them.

(6b) Tell me what decided you to get in touch with PDS and then with me.

(6c) I don't know what decided me about Girton.

(6d) This finally decided Godwin that he could no longer reconcile his beliefs with his vocation.

영작문제 :

a. 나는 결국 회의에 참석하기로(*attend*) 결정했다.

b. 우리는 무엇을 해야 할지 결정할 수 없었다.

c. 홈런 한방이 그 경기의 결과를 결정했다.

d. 나는 어떤 쪽을 택해야(*choose*) 할지 모르겠다.

e. 그는 그의 아들이 음악가(*musician*)가 될 것을 결정했다. (음악가가 되어야 한다고 결정했다.)

4. determine

[1] determine + Noun

(1a) Demand determines prices.

(1b) The size of the chicken pieces will determine the cooking time.

(1c) The school board determines educational policy.

(1d) A date for the meeting has yet to be determined.

[2] determine (+ wh-pronoun) + to-infinitive

(2a) I determined to make one last attempt.

(2b) They determined to start early.

(2c) No one has yet determined how to enforce a contract for the Internet.

(2d) He determined to rescue his two countrymen.

[3] determine + Nominal Clause

(3a) Time will determine how much we can do.

(3b) The investigation will determine what really happened.

(3c) I determined that I would ask him outright.

(3d) He tried to determine what had gone wrong.

[4] determine + Noun + to-infinitive

(4a) The accident determined him to be more careful.

(4b) The situation determined him to come forward at once.

[5] be + determined + to-infinitive

: 종종 [determine + oneself + to-infinitive]의 수동태인 'be determined to'의 형태로 '…하기로/되기로 마음먹다'의 의미로 쓰인다.

(5a) He is determined to become a pilot.

(5b) His enemies are determined to ruin him.

(5c) She is determined to become a lawyer.

(5d) She is determined to succeed.

(cf. He is very determined. Age and experience will be determining factors in our choice of candidate.)

[6] Other Usage

(6a) We determined on going at once.

(6b) He is determined on a course of treatment.

(6c) The letter determined him against the plan.

영작문제 :

a. 우리 여행 날짜를 결정하자.

b. 나는 아직 무엇을 해야 할지 결정하지 않았다.

c. 그의 격려(*his encouragement*)가 나로 하여금 실험을 계속 진행하도록(*go on with the experiment*) 결심하게 하였다.

d. 그녀는 그 선거에서 승리할 것을 마음먹었다.

e. 결국 Magic Johnson의 1초를 남긴(*with just one second left*) 클러치 숏(*clutch shot*)이 경기를 결정지었다.

5. happen

[1] happen + ø (+ Preposition(to)…)

(1a) What is happening?

(1b) Trouble always seems to happen when he's around.

(1c) He trotted to the truck and switched on the ignition. Nothing happened.

(1d) The accident happened close to Martha's Vineyard.

(1e) What happened to the car keys?

(1f) What has happened to him?

(1g) What will happen to the business when the owner retires?

[2] happen + to−infinitive

(2a) I just happened to be in the wrong place at the wrong time.

(2b) We happened to discover we had a friend in common.

(2c) The bus station happens to be close to the museum.

(2d) I happen to know the answer to that question.

[3] There + happen + to−be…

: 종종 '우연히 …가 있(었)다'의 의미로 'there is−구문'과 'happen to−구문'이 합쳐져서 'there happen to be−구문'이 사용된다.

(3a) There happened to be a policeman on the corner, so I asked him the way.

(3b) There happened to be a post office in the next street.

[4] It + happens + Nominal Clause

: 'It happens that…'의 가주어 구문으로 쓰여 뒤의 명사절의 내용이 우연히 일어난 것을 의미한다.

(4a) It happens that I'm married into a German family.

(4b) It happened that she was out when we called.

영작문제 :

a. 당신에게 어떤 일이든 일어날 수 있다.

b. 나는 우연히 그녀를 백화점에서 만났다.

c. 일어나 보니(*when I woke up*) (우연히도) 아름다운 꽃들이 내 옆에 있었다.

6. earn

[1] earn + Noun (+ Preposition(for)…)

(1a) He earns $200 a day.

(1b) She earned a gold medal for swimming.

(1c) Take a day off; you've earned it.

(1d) He earned a Ph.D. in chemistry.

(1e) He earned a reputation for being very thoughtful.

[2] earn + Noun + Noun

(2a) Oil exports earned the nation millions of dollars.

(2b) His latest book earned him worldwide acclaim.

(2c) I think that's earned her very high admiration.

(2d) His outstanding ability earned him a place on the team.

영작문제 :

a. 기업들은 정직한 회사라는 명성(*a reputation for honesty*)을 얻어야 한다.

b. 그의 행동(*His action*)이 그에게 전 세계로부터 칭찬(*praise*)을 받게 했다. (그의 행동으로 그는 전 세계의 칭찬을 받았다.)

c. 그의 승리가 그에게 $1,000을 가져다주었다. (그는 승리한 대가로 $1,000을 벌었다.)

7. get

[1] get + Adjective

(1a) The boys were getting bored.

(1b) He gets angry and aggressive and then he feels guilty.

(1c) Let's hurry. It is getting late.

[2] get + Particle(Preposition/Adverb)···

(2a) How did we get into this recession, and what can we do to get out of it?

(2b) If you get into trouble, there will be police officers to come to your assistance.

(2c) Generally I get to work at 9:30.

(2d) It was dark by the time she got home(Adverb).

(2e) You can get from Reading to Swindon in 30 minutes by train.

(2f) The talks are getting nowhere and they want to withdraw.

(2g) I got to the point where I was so ill I was waiting to die.

(2h) Should I get my money back?

(2i) Please get in.

(2j) They tried to get in touch with her.

[3] get + to-infinitive

(3a) I never ever get to finish my lunch.

(3b) They got to stay in nice hotels.

(3c) Do you get to see him often?

(3d) No one could figure out how he got to be so wealthy.

(3e) Miller and Gabriel got to be friends.

[4] get + Noun (+ Preposition…)

(4a) I want to get a job in New York.

(4b) The winner of the quiz gets a free Christmas Holiday in Jamaica.

(4c) To get a mortgage I got myself a proper job.

(4d) What really gets(annoys) me is his total indifference.

(4e) Go get(bring) your daddy for me.

(4f) I tried to get her to bed.

(4g) She gets enormous pleasure out of working freelance.

(4h) I would like to take pictures professionally because I get so much out of it.

[5] get + Noun + Noun

(5a) I asked him to get me some information.

(5b) Get me a napkin, please.

(5c) Get him a large box.

(5d) To get a mortgage I got myself a proper job.

[6] get + Noun + to-infinitive/Adjective/-ing/-ed

(6a) How did you get him to pose for this picture?

(6b) Why don't you get your friend to help you?

(6c) It is very important that you should get everybody in that community involved.

(6d) He had gotten something stuck between her teeth.

(6e) It almost got him seriously disciplined, and maybe even expelled from the school.

(6f) It is never too late to get the adrenalin flowing through the body again.

(6g) Get them ready for the game.

[7] get + V-ing

(7a) It's getting dark, so let's get moving.

(7b) We need to get thinking, talking, and acting on this before it is too late.

[8] Other Usage

(8a) I've got to do something to stop this pain.

(8b) I don't get how guys dress today.

(8c) I don't get it. What is the problem with her?

(8d) I don't get it. What do you mean?

(8e) We are getting used to his behaviors.

Grammar Tip 1 : 불변화사와 구동사

여기서 particle(불변화사)이란 전치사나 부사가 동사와 함께 쓰여서 구동사(phrasal verb)를 구성하는 경우에 해당 전치사와 부사를 일반적인 전치사 또는 부사와 구분하여 부르는 명칭이다. 이 때 particle이 동사와 함께 쓰여 동사의 보조적 역할을 하게 되는데 그 결과 자동사를 타동사로 쓸 수 있도록 만들거나 의미를 다양하게 표현하는 역할 등을 하게 된다. 또한 명사를 목적어로 갖는 일반 전치사와 달리 때때로 구동사의 전치사 뒤에는 문장이 오기도 한다. 이런 점에서 때, 장소, 이유 등의 일반적인 부사적 기능을 하는 전치사와 구분된다.

영작문제 :

a. 그 아이들은(*the boys*) 지루해지고 있었다.

b. 먹을 것 좀 가져다줄까(*Do/Would you want me to…, Should I…*)?
(뭐 먹을 것 좀 가져다주길 원하니?)

c. 너 그 사람 자주 보게 되니?

d. 나는 너를 곤란한 상황(*trouble*)에 처하게 하고 싶지 않다.

e. 우리는 Jane이 이 서류에 사인하도록 했다.

f. 보통 나는 7:00에 직장에 도착한다.

g. 그녀가 집에 왔을 때는(*by the time*) 이미 그들은 떠나고 없었다(*they had gone away*).

8. make

[1] make + Noun (+ Preposition…)

(1a) She made her own bread.

(1b) Everyone was making money.

(1c) We are making a film about wildlife.

(1d) I keep making the same mistakes.

(1e) He makes a living as a stand–up comic.

(1f) You've made a terrible mess of this job.

(1g) I easily make friends with people.

(1h) He made his first team debut against his beloved Rangers at Ibrox.

(1i) At that stage we had to make a decision on the matter.

(1j) This enables enterprising foreign industrialists to make money out of our ideas.

(1k) These shoes weren't made for walking.

[2] make + Noun + Noun

(2a) He made her his wife.

(2b) The role of James Bond made him a star.

(2c) She made us all coffee.

(2d) The role made him a star.

(2e) She made him her assistant.

[3] make + Noun + ø −Infinitive/Adjective/−ing/−ed

(3a) It made her look younger.

(3b) You're making yourself ridiculous.

(3c) She made life very difficult for me.

(3d) Their votes made it possible for him to assert he won outright.

(3e) The news made him very happy.

(3f) He made it clear that he objected.

(3g) Harry Truman had made it back to Washington just in time for this historic occasion.

(3h) I can't speak Polish but I made myself understood.

(3i) He almost had to shout to make himself heard about the music.

(3j) You made them laugh.

(3k) They live in a fantasy world which makes Euro Disney seem uninventive.

(3l) Her behavior makes even Sarah appear angelic.

(3m) Parents must be made to feel more responsible.

(3n) I was made to feel guilty and irresponsible.

[4] Other Usage

(4a) People just don't know what to make of the news coming from China.

(4b) We made it into a beautiful home.

(4c) She will make a good actress if she gets the right training.

(4d) Phrasal verbs : make for, make of, make off, make out, make over, make up, make up for, make up to, etc.

영작문제 :

a. 그의 행동이 그녀를 화나게 했다.

b. 그는 그의 자식들에게 유산을 물려주지 않을(*leave his money to his children*) 것을 확실하게 했다.

c. 그는 그의 아들을 변호사로 만들었다.

d. 그는 나무로(*out of wood*) 상자를 만들었다.

e. 너는 훌륭한 작가가 될 것이다.

f. 그들은 가까스로(*barely*) 마지막 기차를 탔다.

9. keep

[1] keep + Noun

(1a) I was able to keep control of my emotion.

(1b) He had kept his secrets.

(1c) I would never keep a vicious dog!

(1d) He used to keep the shop down here.

(1e) You can hand things to the staff and they'll keep them for you.

(1f) Keep the change.

(1g) You're an hour late—what kept you?

[2] keep + Adjective/−ing/−ed/Preposition…(Adjectival Phrase)

(2a) She wanted to tell them to stop their noise, but she kept quiet.

(2b) I always swim, and I try to keep healthy.

(2c) We huddled together to keep warm.

(2d) Please keep focused on this paper.

(2e) For several years I kept in touch with her.

[3] keep + (on) V–ing(Gerund)

(3a) Keep smiling!

(3b) I keep forgetting.

(3c) My mother keeps asking when I'm going to get a boyfriend.

(3d) Her clothes kept shrinking more each time they were washed.

(3e) I turned back after a while, but he kept walking.

(3f) Don't keep on interrupting me.

[4] keep + Noun + Adjective/–ing/–ed/Preposition···(Adjectival Phrase)

(4a) The noise kept him awake.

(4b) I'm very sorry to keep you waiting.

(4c) She kept the children amused for hours.

(4d) If you keep a room white and uncluttered it makes it seem lighter and bigger.

(4e) From caffeine to kitchenware to my laptop: these things keep my life running smoothly.

(4f) They kept him in the prison in Berlin.

(4g) He kept his coat on.

(4h) He kept his head down.

(4i) They were keeping Reggie busy behind the bar.

(4j) Reggie was being kept busy behind the bar.

[5] keep + from + V–ing

: '…하지 않으려 하다, 금지하다, …하지 못하게 하다'는 의미로 쓰일 때 전치사 'from'과 함께 쓰인다. 이는 유사한 의미의 다른 동사들(to prevent, to bar, to stop)의 경우에도 마찬가지이다.

(5a) He had to lean on Dan to keep from falling.

(5b) She bit her lip to keep from crying.

(5c) It is not clear if the country can keep from sliding back into the economic crisis.

[6] keep + Noun(something) + from + Noun(somebody)

(6a) She knew that Gabriel was keeping something from her.

(6b) They tried to keep the news from their grandfather.

(6c) But keeping the secret from my mother was the greater burden.

[7] keep + Noun + from + V–ing

(7a) Can eating too much fruit keep me from losing weight?

(7b) He kept her from being lonely.

(7c) To keep your wife from leaving, it is vital that you not only hear your wife but you pay attention to her.

[8] Other Usage

(8a) When you get news, do you keep it to yourself?

(8b) How are you keeping these days?

(8c) Phrasal Verbs : keep at, keep down, keep in with, keep on, keep on about, keep on at, keep to, keep up, keep up with, etc.

영작문제 :

a. 나는 계속 몸을 따뜻하게 했다.

b. Michelle은 그가 진실을 알지 못하게 하고 있다.

c. 소음(*The noise*)이 그를 계속 깨어 있게 했다. (그는 소음 때문에 깨어 있었다.)

d. 그는 우리를 역에서 세 시간동안 계속 기다리게 했다.

e. 이 dress 내가 갖아도 되나요?

f. 나는 그가 저녁을 먹지 못하게 하고 있었다.

g. 그의 격려가 나를 계속하게/나아가게(*go*) 만든다.

h. 의사들은 그녀를 병원에 계속 있게 할 것이다. (계속 입원하게 할 것이다.)

10. prevent

[1] prevent + Noun

(1a) Lotion or cream is effective as sunscreen agent to prevent sunburn.

(1b) The accident could have been prevented.

[2] prevent + Noun + (from) V-ing

(2a) Further treatment will prevent cancer from developing.

(2b) Nothing would prevent him from speaking out against injustice.

(2c) Industry should spend the money to prevent accidents from happening in the first place.

(2d) He is prevented by law from holding a licence.

(2e) The police have been trying to prevent them carrying weapons.

(2f) The plastic lining prevents alkaline water seeping into the hole.

(2g) Nothing would prevent him/his speaking out against injustice.

영작문제 :

a. Jane의 부모는 그녀가 파티에 가지 못하게 했다.

b. 국민들은(*Its nationals*) 그 나라를 떠나지(*leave the country*) 못하게 금지될 수 있다.

11. stop

[1] stop + ø

(1a) The car stopped at the traffic lights.

(1b) When he stopped abruptly, I nearly collided with him.

(1c) When it comes to working out, do you know when to stop?

(1d) His heart stopped three times.

(1e) Let' stop for lunch now.

(1f) We stopped at an inn for dinner.

(1g) People just don't stop to think about the consequences.

(1h) She criticizes everyone and the trouble is, she doesn't know when to stop.

[2] stop + Noun

(2a) He stopped his car at the big stone posts.

(2b) No one can stop me.

(2c) He was stopped by the police for speeding.

(2d) Stop me if I'm boring you.

(2e) Mike immediately stopped what he was doing.

[3] stop + V-ing

(3a) We should stop worrying about things we can't control.

(3b) Izzy had decided to stop drinking.

(3c) That phone never stops ringing.

(3d) Please stop crying and tell me what's wrong.

[4] stop + Noun + (from) V-ing

(4a) Motherhood won't stop me from pursuing my acting career.

(4b) There's nothing to stop you from working on this project.

(4c) I think she really would have liked to stop us seeing each other.

(4d) He put the radio on loud to stop himself thinking about it.

(4e) You can't stop people saying what they think.

[5] Other Usage

(5a) There's no stopping us now.

(5b) She stopped dead in her tracks but did not turn to face him.

(5c) They will not stop short of assassination.

영작문제 :

a. 기차는 역에 섰다.

b. 그는 노래 부르는 것을 멈추었다.

c. 우리는 쉬기 위해서 멈추었다.

d. Jane의 부모는 그녀가 파티에 가지 못하게 막았다.

12. learn

[1] learn + Ø

(1a) The best way to learn is to learn for yourself.

(1b) The book is about how children learn.

[2] learn + Preposition…

(2a) She needed to learn about speaking verse.

(2b) Sylvia tries to learn from William about leadership and addressing groups.

(2c) Of course you always learn by your mistakes.

(2d) Your child will also learn from watching you.

(2e) I've been wanting to tell you how much I think we can learn from you.

(2f) I learned of her arrival from a close friend.

(2g) I'm sure she'll learn from her mistakes.

(2h) He had learned of his father's death in Australia.

[3] learn + Noun

(3a) Their children are going to learn English.

(3b) Before he could answer those questions, Ryan knew that he'd have to learn the facts.

(3c) I had to learn the new computer program.

(3d) I learned the lesson the hard way.

[4] learn + (wh−pronoun) to−infinitive

(4a) He is learning to play the piano.

(4b) He's learning to dance.

(4c) Today we learned how to use the new software.

(4d) It is much better if we can learn to be more open about our emotional responses.

(4e) Managers and operators learn from experience how to operate new technologies.

(4f) I soon learned not to ask too many questions.

[5] learn + Nominal Clause

(5a) She learned that her grandmother had been a nurse.

(5b) Russia has learned from experience that political struggle has no future.

(5c) You sort of learn where your destructive emotional behavior is coming from and what motivates it.

(5d) We only learned who the new teacher was a few days ago.

영작문제 :

a. 우리는 역사를 통해서 미래를 배울 수 있다.

b. 나는 Dean이 음악에 재능이 있다는 사실을 알게 되었다.

c. 그의 미소를 통해서(*from his smile*) 내가 시험에 합격했다는 사실을 알았다.

13. maintain

[1] maintain + Noun

(1a) They have always maintained their innocence.

(1b) The government will maintain tight control over the money supply.

(1c) He maintained his opposition to the plan.

[2] maintain + Nominal Clause

(2a) He maintains that he didn't know what he was carrying.
(2b) They maintain that he had nothing to do with drugs.
(2c) He maintained that the earth was round.

영작문제 :

a. Paul은 자신의 무죄(*innocence*)를 주장했다.
b. 우리는 법과 질서(*law and order*)를 유지해야 한다.
c. 그들은 자신들이 경기를 이겼다고 주장했다.

14. name

[1] name + Noun (+ Preposition(after, for, as, etc.)…)

(1a) Can you name the capital of Ohio?
(1b) Three persons were named in the report.
(1c) We need to name the time for our meeting.
(1d) They named each room after famous artists.
(1e) I have named you for the position.
(1f) The couple named their child after both grandparents.
(1g) The San Francisco Giants became the first team to name a black man as their manager.
(1h) They also named a locomotive for him.

[2] name + Noun + Noun (+ Preposition(after, for, as, etc.)⋯)

(2a) He named his horse Speedy.
(2b) She named the child Edward.
(2c) I named her Salish after one of the Indian tribes from the south.
(2d) They named him Shankly as a mark of respect for their former manager.
(2e) She was named after her mother.
(2f) I was very surprised when I was asked if I would have a rose named after me.

영작문제 :

a. 그들은 그를 작은 거인(*the little giant*)이라고 불렀다.
b. 그 부부는 자신들의 딸을 할머니의 이름을 따서 Peggy라고 했다.

15. offer

[1] offer + Noun (+ Preposition⋯)

(1a) I can't offer an explanation for that.
(1b) The team will start offering contracts to its players next week.
(1c) He offered the painting to me at a reduced price.
(1d) Those boots are being offered at half price.
(1e) The house is being offered at 1.5 million dollars.
(1f) The hotel offers magnificent views over the lake.

[2] offer + to-infinitive

(2a) She offered to accompany me.

(2b) We did not offer to go first.

(2c) He offered to take her home in a taxi.

(2d) I offered to answer any questions.

(2e) I offered to pay for her.

[3] offer + Noun + Noun

(3a) He offered me a seat.

(3b) He offered me a chocolate and I shook my head.

(3c) Can I offer you something to drink?

(3d) I offered her a fair price for the land.

(3e) She offered him emotional and practical support in countless ways.

(3f) They are offered very little counselling or support.

영작문제 :

a. 우리는 여러분께 양질의 서비스(*a quality service*)를 제공하고 있습니다.

b. Peter는 그들에게 수상스키 타는 법을 가르쳐주겠다고(*teach them waterskiing*) 제의했습니다.

c. 나는 많은 돈을 제의받았다.

16. pay

[1] pay + Ø

(1a) I haven't actually paid.

(1b) Crime doesn't pay.

(1c) It pays to be courteous.

(1d) The murderer paid with his life.

(1e) It doesn't pay to get angry.

(1f) My company pays well.

(1g) Are you paying in cash or by credit card?

[2] pay + Noun

: 'pay'가 타동사로 쓰여 종종 'pay a N'의 형태로 숙어적으로 사용된다.

(2a) Please pay your bill.

(2b) I paid my rent.

(2c) She paid her dues in small-town theaters before being cast in a Broadway play.

(2d) But it paid him in the long run.

(2e) We paid a visit to him.

(2f) She paid a call on him.

(2g) Please pay attention to me!

[3] pay + Preposition(for)…

(3a) You'll pay for this mischief!

(3b) He paid for the insult with a blow.

(3c) Roberto paid for the tickets.

(3d) They made him pay dearly for that.

[4] pay + Noun + Preposition(for)…

(4a) He paid twenty dollars for the shirt.

(4b) He paid me for my work.

(4c) You should be paid for the work you do.

(4d) That's what you are paid for.

(4e) She pays $400 a week for this apartment.

[5] pay + Noun + Noun

(5a) We had to pay the man the money because that's the going rate for the job.

(5b) Helen has suddenly decided to pay Carmela a visit.

(5c) He still hasn't paid me the money he owes.

(5d) I'm paid $100 a day.

[6] Other Usage

(6a) She paid us back by refusing the invitation.

(6b) Your efforts will eventually pay off.

(6c) How can we ever pay you back for what you've done for us?

(6d) They paid for her to go.

(6e) Her parents paid for her to go to Canada.

영작문제 :

a. 네가 받은 훈련(*your training*)이 장래에(*in the future*) 네게 도움이 될 것이다.

b. 그는 신용카드(*credit card*)로 계산을 했다(계산서(*the bill*)를 지불했다).

c. 다음번 서울에 오게 되면(*next time you are in Seoul*) 저희를 방문해 주세요.

d. 나는 그 햄버거 값으로 $10을 지불했다.

e. 그들은 내게 $500을 지불했다.

f. 나는 $500을 받았다.

17. say

[1] say + Noun (+ Preposition…)

(1a) What did you say? I said "Hello!"

(1b) I was sure Johnny said that.

(1c) Henry walked by without saying a word.

(1d) She said nothing to me about it.

(1e) What does the election say about the mood of voters in Massachusetts?

(1f) I wouldn't say no to a drink.

(1g) It says much for his understanding English literature.

(1h) His angry glance said it all.

(1i) The clock said three o'clock.

[2] say + Nominal clause

(2a) He said that he would resign. (⇐ He said, "I will resign.")

(2b) They cannot say who the captured men are. (⇐ "Who are the captured men?")

(2c) He said his name was Sam.

(2d) She finds it hard to say what she feels

(2e) Someone recently said to me that there are no atheists, that we all worship some god.

(2f) The book doesn't say where he was born.

(2g) The instructions say we should leave it to set for four hours.

[3] It is said that…

: 위의 (2)번 문장들의 경우 일반적인 주어(they, we)가 쓰일 때 종종 가주어 'it'와 함께 수동으로 쓰인다. (⇐ They(People) say that… We say that…)

(3a) It is said that she lived to be over 100.

(3b) It is often said that the next war in the Middle East will not be about oil but water.

(3c) It is said that Tom is a good painter.

[4] Other Usage

(4) The guidebook says to turn left.

Grammar Tip 2 : Subject-Raising(주어 올리기)

위의 [3]의 문장들은 다음과 같이 종속절의 주어가 전체문장의 주어로 올라가서 to-부정사와 함께 쓰일 수 있다. 이 때 (3b) 문장처럼 쓰이지 않는다.

(1) She is said to have lived to be over 100.

(2) The next war in the Middle East is said to be not about oil but water.

(3a) Tom is said to be a good painter.

(3b) (X) Tom is said that he is a liar.

영작문제 :

a. 그 배우는 자신의 대사(*his lines*)를 완벽하게 말했다.

b. 그는 나를 다시 보고 싶다고 말했다.

c. 그는 자신이 무엇을 할지 말하지 않았다.

d. 그 단어는 무엇을 말하는가(뜻하는가)?

e. i) 그들은 Paul이 거짓말쟁이라고 말한다.

ii) Paul이 거짓말쟁이라고 하더라. (그들에 의해 말해지다.) : it을 주어로 하는 수동태문장

iii) ii)와 같은 수동태의 의미로 Paul을 주어로 하는 경우

18. tell

[1] tell + Noun(Direct Object)

: '…을 말하다'의 의미로 일반적인 타동사로 직접목적어가 오는 경우에 해당된다.

(1a) To tell the truth, I don't think much of psychiatrists.

(1b) I'll tell it to you someday.

(1c) We told a lot of lies.

(1d) Many hours had passed when Karen finished telling her story to Kim.

[2] tell + Noun(Indirect Object) (+ Preposition(about, of)…)

: '…에게 말하다'의 의미로 간접목적어가 오는 경우이다. 종종 위의 [1]에서 목적어였던 특정 화제 혹은 주제에 관하여 말할 때 전치사 'about, of'와 함께 쓰인다.

(2a) I told you so.

(2b) He told us of his dream to sail around the world.

(2c) A : Then how do you know she's well?

B : She told me so.

(2d) She told me about a dream in which she had seen someone who looked like her.

(2e) She tried to keep it a secret and didn't want to tell us about losing the child.

(2f) Why wasn't I told about the accident? (⇐ Why didn't you(they) tell me about the accident? : 또한 수동태의 경우 보통 '듣다/듣지 못하다'의 의미로 쓰임.)

[3] tell + Noun + Noun

: 간접목적어와 직접목적어가 다 사용되는 경우이다.

(3a) Will you tell me a story?

(3b) Please tell me the reason.

(3c) Tell me the truth.

(3d) She told him the news.

(3e) I never told her a thing.

(3f) Do what I tell you.

[4] tell + Noun + Nominal Clause

(4a) Ingrid told Peter that he should go ahead. (⇐ Ingrid told Peter, "You should go ahead.")

(4b) Can you tell us if there's any truth to that?

(4c) The facts tells us that this is not true.

(4d) Tell me what happened.

(4e) She told him that the store was closed.

(4f) He told me that he was a farmer.

(4g) I told her what the doctor had said.

(4h) It is told that ice turns into gas in space upon exposure to sufficiently strong sunlight. (⇐ They tell us that ice turns into gas in space upon exposure to sufficiently strong sunlight.)

[5] Subject + be told + that…

: [4]의 'A tells B that…'의 문장은 종종 간접목적어인 B가 주어가 되어 'B is told that…'의 수동문장으로 쓰이곤 하며 이 때 'be told'는 '…을 듣다'를 의미한다.

(5a) I am told that your name is John. Is that correct? (⇐ They tell me that your name is John.)

(5b) I was told that I could go to the embassy and get my visa. (⇐ They told me that I could go to the embassy and get my visa.)

[6] can/can't tell + Noun/Nominal clause

: 조동사(Auxiliary Verb) 'can/can't'와 함께 쓰여 '알 수 있다/알 수 없다'의 의미로 쓰인다.

(6a) You can't really tell the difference between their policies and ours.

(6b) I could tell that he was really worried.

(6c) We could tell that he was upset.

(6d) I couldn't tell if he had been in a fight or had just fallen down.

(6e) When you look at this photography you can tell he loved his subjects.

(6f) He can usually tell what people want by talking to them.

(6g) You could tell by their eyes if they had been smoking.

(6h) He could almost tell by looking at it whether a machine would fly well or not.

(6i) You can tell he's joking.

[7] tell + Noun + to-infinitive

: 목적어와 목적보어와 함께 쓰여 '…에게 …하라고 말하다/조언하다/충고하다/지시하다' 등의 의미로 쓰인다. 이때도 수동태로 자주 쓰인다.

(7a) He told her to remain at the villa.

(7b) She told the customers to wait in line.

(7c) I told her to send the letter by airmail.

(7d) There was a sign telling motorists to slow down.

(7e) She was told to remain at the villa and was quite happy to do so. (⇐ They told her to remain at the villa…)

(7f) He was told to sit down and wait. (⇐ They told him to sit down and wait.)

[8] tell + Noun +wh−pronoun + to−infinitive

(8a) Don't tell me what to do.

(8b) They didn't tell us what to do with the result.

[9] (can/can't) tell A from B

: 전치사 'from'과 함께 쓰여 'A와 B를 구분할 수 있다/없다'의 의미로 쓰인다.

(9a) He lost the ability to tell truth from fiction.

(9b) How do you tell one from another?

(9c) He couldn't tell chalk from cheese.

(9d) Can you tell Tom from his twin brother?

[10] Other Usage

(10a) Children must do as they're told.

(10b) As far as I can tell, she's enjoying the course.

(10c) It sounds like nonsense to me, but I can't tell.

(10d) A: That's not an original.

B: How can you tell?

(10e) It's difficult to tell them apart.

(10f) He told her of how the paramedics arrived when he had the seizure.

(10g) At last she told Paul of what she had seen.

영작문제 :

a. 나에게 당신의 이름과 주소를 말해 주세요.

b. 그는 나에게 학교로 돌아가라고 말했다.

c. 그는 내게 그 소식(*the news*)을 말했다.

d. 아무도 그 이유를 말할 수 없다(모른다).

e. 그는 내게 자신의 어린 시절에 대해 이야기했다.

f. 의사는 나에게 걱정하지 말라고 했다.

g. 우리는 그림을 만지지 말라고 지시받았다.

h. 그녀는 나에게 주말동안 감기로 아팠었다고 말했다.

i. 우리는 그녀가 주말동안 감기로 아팠었다는 말을 들었다.

j. 나는 그가 기쁜지 아닌지 알 수 없었다.

k. 그녀는 현실(*reality*)과 허구(*fiction*)를 구분 못한다.

19. talk

[1] talk + ø

(1a) The boys all began to talk at once.

(1b) We talked for hours.

(1c) The baby can talk.

(1d) The parrot talks.

[2] talk + Preposition…

(2a) I talked to him yesterday.

(2b) The candidate talked about the pros and cons of the issue.

(2c) He intends to talk to young people about the dangers of AIDS.

(2d) He briefly talked on the history of the city.

(2e) The article talks about the latest fashions.

(2f) I talked with the doctor.

(2g) I enjoyed talking to Anna.

[3] Other Usage

(3a) Lets talk business.

(3b) The police found money in the car. We're talking significant amounts of money.

(3c) The passenger talked French with the flight crew.

(3d) Can you talk the local dialect?

(종종 명사형을 이용하여)

(3e) We had a nice talk over lunch.

(3f) He gave a talk on art.

(3g) There is talk of bankruptcy.

영작문제 :

a. 우리는 밤새도록 영화에 대해 이야기했다.

b. 그녀는 George와 환경문제(*environmental issues*)에 대해 이야기하였다.

20. take

[1] take + Noun (+ Preposition…(Adverbial Phrase))

(1a) Here, let me take your coat.

(1b) He has taken my money, and I have no chance of getting it back.

(1c) The storm took its toll.

(1d) Your remark took me by surprise.

(1e) Don't forget to take your umbrella.

(1f) Our team took the visitors three to one.

(1g) I'll take these papers home and read them.

(1h) A combination of talent, hard work and good looks have taken her to the top.

(1i) This bus will take you to Dallas.

(1j) The guide took us to the waterfall.

(1k) She took a deep breath.

(1l) I'll take your word that he's telling the truth.

[2] It + takes + Noun + to-infinitive

(2a) It only takes a few minutes to wash the car.

(2b) It takes 15 minutes to convert the plane into a car by removing the wings and the tail.

(2c) It takes money to live in this town.

[3] Other Usage : take + Preposition(Particle)

take after, take away, take back, take down, take for, take in, take off, take on, take over, take up, etc.

영작문제 :

a. 나는 이번 학기에 세 과목을 듣는다.

b. Cathy는 10년 동안 수면제(*sleeping pills*)를 복용해 왔다.

c. 카메라 가져가는 것 잊지 말아라(*Don't forget to*…).

d. 그는 내게서 자신감(*confidence*)을 가져가 버렸다.

e. 서울에서 부산까지 KTX로 약 3시간이 걸린다.

21. wait

[1] wait + ø

(1a) We just have to wait and see what happens.

(1b) Lunch is waiting at the counter.

(1c) The trip will have to wait.

(1d) If you think this all sounds very exciting, just wait until you read the book.

(1e) Please wait here until he is ready to see you.

[2] wait + Preposition(for)···

(2a) There was a message waiting for him in his box.
(2b) I waited for five minutes for Ann.
(2c) I can't wait for your next letter.
(2d) If he's late, I'll wait for him.
(2e) A letter is waiting for you.
(2f) I stayed at home, waiting for her call.

[3] wait + for Noun + to-infinitive

: 이 구문에서는 'wait for'가 하나의 타동사처럼, 즉 구동사로 쓰여 목적어와 목적보어를 갖는다고 볼 수 있다.

(3a) He would then always wait for other people to make up his mind for him.
(3b) She had to wait for 20 minutes for Ian to find his keys.
(3c) She waited for me to say something.
(3d) They can't wait for us to go.
(3e) They waited for him to finish
(3f) I waited for Dad to come home.
(3g) I'm waiting for them to make a decision.

[4] wait + to-infinitive

(4a) I can't wait to find out what it was all about.
(4b) They couldn't wait to get back inside.

(4c) I can't wait to see his face

[5] Other Usage

(5a) Murphy wasn't afraid, but ready for action, waiting his chance. (to await)

(5b) They waited lunch for us. (시중들다, waiter & waitress)

(5c) The tall girl is waiting tables.

(5d) Don't wait supper for me.

(5e) There are plenty of servants to wait on her.

(5f) They waited lunch for us. (to postpone)

영작문제 :

a. 기다리게 해서 미안해(*Sorry to keep you…*).

b. 우리는 그를 하루 종일 기다리고 있다.

c. 우리는 비가 그치기를 기다리고 있다.

d. 네 휴가(*vacation*)는 좀 있어야 갈 수 있다(기다려야 한다).

22. accuse

[1] accuse + Noun + Preposition(of, for, as)…

(1a) You don't have to accuse him of anything.

(1b) They accused her of making mistakes.

(1c) The president accused his government of scandalous corruption and incompetence.

(1d) They accused him for his selfishness.

(1e) She accused Jim as an accomplice.

(1f) He accused them of drinking beer while driving.

(1g) They accused him of stealing the car.

[2] be + accused + of…

(2a) Her assistant was accused of theft and fraud by the police.

(2b) He is accused of killing ten young women.

(2c) He was accused of stealing the car.

(2d) The youths were accused of robbery.

(2e) We saw the trial of a party of youths accused of robbery.

영작문제 :

a. 그들은 그가 거짓말을 했다고 비난했다.

b. 그들은 그를 인종차별로(인종차별을 했다고) 비난했다.

c. 그는 인종차별로 비난 받았다.

23. encourage

[1] encourage + Noun (+ Preposition…)

(1a) The general tried to encourage the troops.

(1b) You should not encourage him in his extravagance.

(1c) The school encourages all sorts of athletic sports.

(1d) Investors were encouraged by the news.

(1e) Participation is encouraged at all levels.

(1f) I was encouraged by his praise.

(1g) She encouraged him with friendly advice.

(1h) She encouraged him in his work.

[2] encourage + Noun + to-infinitive

(2a) He encouraged her to make another attempt.

(2b) Letters of support encouraged the mayor to run again.

(2c) You must encourage him to try again.

(2d) He encouraged her to quit her job.

영작문제 :

a. 그는 시련 기간 동안 내내(*throughout the ordeal*) 친절한 말로(*with kind words*) 그녀를 격려했다.

b. 우리는 대중의 긍정적인 반응(*the positive response of the public*)에 크게 고무되었다.

c. 선생님은 그녀를 권장하여 단편소설(*short stories*)을 쓰게 했다. (그녀가 단편소설을 쓰도록 권장하였다)

d. 우리는 외국어를 공부하도록 격려되었다.

e. 체벌(*corporal punishment*)은 아이들 사이에 폭력(*violence*)을 조장한다.

24. give

[1] give + Noun (+ Preposition(to)…)

(1a) I gave five dollars for the book.

(1b) Cows give milk.

(1c) He gave the letter to the teacher.

(1d) Hold the bride's bouquet during the service and give it to the bride to carry in the procession down the aisle.

[2] give + Noun + Noun

(2a) You can always give me some money.

(2b) That gave me the advantage.

(2c) We gave her flowers for her birthday.

(2d) Give him some cough medicine.

(2e) Give us the latest news.

(2f) The teacher gave us an hour to finish.

(2g) He gave the door a push.

(2h) Ana gave Bal's hand a squeeze.

(2i) No one has given her the praise and recognition.

(2j) They went for walks together in the fields and gave each other language lessons.

(2k) He gave the crowd the trophy for winning the race.

(2l) The man was given life imprisonment for the crime.

[3] give + a Noun

(3a) She gave a little laugh.

(3b) He gave a short speech.

[4] Other Usage

give up, give in, give away, give back, give out, etc.

영작문제 :

a. 이 편지를 너의 어머니께 드려라.

b. 나는 그에게 $200을 주었다.

c. 그는 결심을 하도록 내게 일주일(*a week to decide*)을 주었다. (결심하기 위한 일주일을 내게 주었다.)

d. 나는 결심을 할 일주일을 부여받았다.

25. like

[1] like + Ø

(1a) Get a glass, if you like.

(1b) Stay if you like.

[2] like + Noun

(2a) I like your style.

(2b) She liked the film.

(2c) I would like some coffee.

(2d) I don't like the position I'm in.

(2e) How do you like these new theater seats?

(2f) I'd like a piece of cake.

(2g) Would you like some tea?

(2h) What music do you like best?

[3] like + to-infinitive

(3a) She likes to sing.

(3b) I like to read.

(3c) He likes to hear music.

[4] like + V-ing

(4a) I like going to the cinema.

(4b) I don't like seeing our people killed.

(4c) I like reading.

(4d) I just don't like being in crowds.

(4e) He likes boxing.

[5] would like + to-infinitive

: 'like to'로 쓰일 때는 '…하는 것을/…하기 좋아하다'의 의미로 사용되지만 'would like to'는 '…하고 싶다'의 의미를 갖는다.

(5a) Where would you like to go for dinner?

(5b) I would like to thank Captain Peter Golden who organized the voyage for me.

(5c) Would you like to meet him?

[6] would like + Noun + to-infinitive

(6a) I'd like you to consider this matter.

(6b) I would like you to come to my party.

(6c) Mr. Lee said there were a few questions he would like Mr. Baker to answer.

(6d) I'd like you to tell them where I am.

[7] Other Usage

(7a) The guests don't like it when they can't use the pool.

(7b) How would you like it if people followed you round all the time?

(7c) How would you like it if somebody did the same to you?

(7d) I'd like it if we were friends again.

(7e) I'd really like it if you sent a letter to me.

(7f) I like it when it snows.

영작문제 :

a. 그는 즉시 떠나고 싶어 한다.

b. 나는 가능한 한 자주 그녀를 방문하고 싶다.

c. 나는 여행하는 것을 좋아한다.

d. 나는 여행하고 싶다.

c. 나는 그가 우리를 방문하기를 바란다.

26. love

[1] love + Noun

(1a) We love our parents.

(1b) Everybody loves a parade.

(1c) The cactus loves hot, dry air.

(1d) He loved his country above all else.

(1e) I love your dress.

[2] love + Noun + Preposition(for)···

(2a) I love you for who you are.

(2b) They loved her for her personality.

(2c) I love him for his generosity.

[3] love + to-infinitive

(3a) I just love to read.

(3b) Angela loved to read children's books with her kids.

[4] love + V-ing

(4a) I love reading his plays.

(4b) I love looking around the shops to see what other retailers are doing and selling.

[5] would love + Noun

: '…를 무척 원하다'의 의미로 쓰인다.

(5a) A : Would you like a drink?

B : I'd love one.

(5b) I'd love a beer.

[6] would love + to-infinitive

: 'would like to'보다 강한 의미로 '무척 …하고 싶다'를 뜻한다.

(6a) I'd love to come.

(6b) A: Would you join our party?

B: I'd love to!

(6c) I would love to earn my own money and not rely on men or benefits.

[7] would love + Noun + to-infinitive

: '…가 …하기를 강하게 원한다'의 의미를 갖는다.

(7a) I would love one of us to go to college.

(7b) I would love him to help us with our project.

(7c) I'd love her to come and live with us.

[8] Other Usage

(8a) She loves men paying her attention.

(8b) She used to love it for us to go and take the children out.

(8c) He is no longer able to love and hate.

영작문제 :

a. 그는 친구들과 이야기하는 것을 매우 좋아한다.

b. 그는 공상 과학 소설 읽는 것을 그 독특함(*peculiarity*) 때문에 무척 좋아한다.

c. 나는 그녀가 우리와 함께 여기에 머무르기를 정말 원한다.

27. desire

[1] desire + Noun

(1a) We all desire health and happiness.

(1b) She had remarried and desired a child with her new husband.

(1c) Her cooking always left much to be desired.

[2] desire + to-infinitive

(2a) We desire to help you in the preparation for the meeting.

(2b) Fewer people desire to live in the cold countries.

(명사로 쓰일 경우 : I have no desire ever to see him again; I have a sudden desire for a bar of chocolate.)

[3] desire + Nominal Clause

(3a) I desire that my dead body should be cremated.

(3b) They desire that he (should) be allowed to leave.

[4] desire + Noun + to-infinitive

(4a) He has desired me to write to him when I go to India.

(4b) I desire a message to be sent to you there.

(4c) His Majesty desires me to make his wishes known to you.

영작문제 :

a. 나는 진정(*dearly*) 행복해지길 원한다.

b. 나는 그들이 그 일을 끝마치길 바란다.

28. hate

[1] hate + Noun

(1a) I don't believe I hate anyone.

(1b) Tapes hate excessive heat.

(1c) Most people hate him, but I don't.

(1d) She hated hospitals and dreaded the operation.

(1e) I hate it when people cry.

[2] hate + Noun + Preposition(for)···

(2a) I hate you for that.

(2b) I do not hate him for not knowing me.

(2c) Don't hate me for this.

(2d) I hate them for their cruelty to my father.

[3] hate + to–infinitive

(3a) I hate to accept it.

(3b) I hate to think you've been unhappy, dear.

(3c) I hate to do this, but let me ask you some tough question.

(3d) I hate to interrupt, but can I ask you a quick question?

(3e) I hate to admit it, but you were right.

(3f) I hate to see him unhappy.

[4] hate + V–ing

(4a) I hate putting my face underwater.

(4b) I hate being tied down to one interest or one philosophy.

(4d) I hate having to commute every day.

(4e) I hate getting up in the morning.

[5] hate + Noun + to–infinitive

(5a) I hate you to talk about it.

(5b) I love cars, and would hate someone to steal mine.

[6] Other Usage

(6a) Listen, I hate for you to go out in the cold.

(6b) I won't do it any more because I hate that people keep asking about it.

(6c) Stop hating on them—they're my friends.

영작문제 :

a. 너를 실망시키기는 정말 싫다.

b. 그 문제 때문에 너를 미워하는 건 아니다.

c. 그는 지기를 정말 싫어한다.

d. 나는 그가 떠나는 것이 정말 싫다.

29. hope

[1] hope + ø

(1a) I sincerely hope so.

(1b) I hope not.

[2] hope + Preposition(for)···

(2a) I just hope for some change for the better.

(2b) Everybody needed something to hope for.

(2c) We are hoping for more financial support.

(2d) We hope for an early spring.

[3] hope + Nominal clause(that)

(3a) The researchers hope that such a vaccine could be available soon.
(3b) We hope the rest of this book will provide the answers to your problems.
(3c) I hope and believe the police will take the strongest possible action.
(3d) I hope that you will join us for dinner.

[4] hope + to-infinitive

(4a) I hope to get a job within the next 2 weeks.
(4b) We hope to buy a house in the spring.
(4c) They hope eventually to develop a new type of painkillers.

영작문제 :

a. 나는 네가 시험에 합격하기를 바란다.
b. 그것이 우리가 희망하던 것이다.
c. Matthew는 내년에 대학원에 진학하기를 희망한다.
d. Matthew의 부모는 내년에 그가 대학원에 진학하기를 희망한다.
e. 나는 최고를 희망하지만 최악의 상황을 준비하고 있다.

30. need

[1] need + Noun

(1a) I've had another job offer, and I need a little time to make up my mind.

(1b) I mean you didn't need a lot of money to support a habit in those days.

(1c) We need your help. (명사로 쓰일 경우, the need for your help)

(1d) What the children need is a bit of discipline.

[2] need + to-infinitive

: 'need not' 다음에는 to-부정사가 생략되어 사용된다. 그러나 일반적으로 'don't need to'가 자주 쓰인다.

(2a) I need to go right now.

(2b) He does not need to worry about money.

(2c) You don't need to shout.

(2d) They need not come.

(2e) You needn't be concerned.

[3] need + Noun + to-infinitive

(3a) I need someone to help me.

(3b) Many women do not necessarily need their husband to provide material security in their lives.

(3c) You'll need someone there to take care of things while you recover.

[4] need + V-ing

: 뒤에 동명사가 올 경우에는 수동의 의미로 쓰인다.

(4a) This car needs fixing. (This car needs to be fixed.)

(4b) The gardens in the neighborhood need tidying up. (The gardens need to be tidied up.)

(4c) This machine needs repairing. (This machine needs to be repaired.)

[5] need + Noun + V-ing

: 여기서도 동명사는 수동의 의미로 사용된다.

(5a) We really need this house redecorating. (We really need this house to be redecorated.)

(5b) Anderson needs his trousers mending. (Anderson needs his trousers to be mended.)

[6] need + Noun + Adjective/-ing/-ed…

(6a) We need Michelle ready for the show.

(6b) I think he needs his head examined if he wants to carry on.

(6c) I need him going after the project.

[7] Other Usage

(7) Need I say more?

영작문제 :

a. 내가 깨 있을 필요가 없다.

b. (나는) 엄마한테 돈을 좀 빌려야겠다.

c. 요리 하는 것 좀 도와줘(…*help me with the cooking*). ('I need'를 사용할 것)

d. 그 shirt는 세탁이 필요하다.

e. 네 머리(*Your hair needs*…) 좀 잘라야겠는데?

31. want

[1] want + ø

(1a) You can wait for him if you want.

(1b) Call me daily if you want.

[2] want + Noun (+ Preposition(for)…)

(2a) Everyone wants something from you now.

(2b) What do they want with stuff like this?

(2c) She wants a glass of water.

(2d) What do you want for your birthday?

(2e) You are wanted by your office.

(2f) The fugitive is wanted by the police.

(2g) They want him in Arizona for armed robbery.

(2h) The man is wanted for questioning in connection with the bombing.

[3] want + to-infinitive

(3a) They want to leave.

(3b) He wants to go home.

(3c) I want to say how really delighted I am.

(3d) If you want to pay by check, please fill in the form below.

(3e) He didn't want to be disturbed during his working time.

(3f) John had been wanting to resign for months.

(3g) I want to ask you a favour, Sara.

(3h) I could do it faster, but I just don't want to.

(3i) He should not be forced to eat it if he doesn't want to.

[4] want + Noun + to-infinitive

(4a) I want you to clean your room.

(4b) I don't want any other mother to be hurt like I have been.

(4c) What do you want me to do?

(4d) They began to want their father to be the same as other daddies.

(4e) I want him to learn to read.

(4f) The little girl wanted me to come and play with her.

[5] want + Noun + Adjective/-ing/-ed

(5a) I want him dead.

(5b) She doesn't want money spent this way.

(5c) I want my son alive.

(5d) I didn't want him around.

(5e) The government doesn't want people drifting to London where they're penniless and homeless.

[6] want + V-ing

: 동명사가 목적어로 올 경우 수동의 의미로 쓰인다.

(6a) Her hair wants cutting.

(6b) His toaster wants repairing, I'm afraid.

(6c) Your shoes want cleaning.

[7] Other Usage

(7a) The cat wants out.

(7b) The dog wants in.

(7c) I want in.

(7d) I don't want you doing that again. Do you understand?

영작문제 :

a. 그는 Italy로 가기를 원한다.

b. 그는 사람들이 그를 쳐다보는 것을 원하지 않았다.

c. 그는 그의 권력(힘)(*power*)을 인정받기(*recognized*)를 원했다.

d. 나는 네가 행복하기를 원한다.

32. wish

[1] wish + ø

(1a) You can go if you wish.

(1b) I will do as you wish.

[2] wish + Preposition(for)…

(2a) I wish for a successful outcome.

(2b) She wishes for a friend.

(2c) They say that they would wish for a neutral and non-aligned Cambodia in the long term.

[3] wish + Nominal Clause (Subjunctive)

: wish는 소망을 나타내는 의미로 쓰여 뒤에 오는 목적절에 현재 사실이나 과거사실의 반대의 의미로 가정법 표현이 오기도 한다.

(3a) I wish I could see you alone.

(3b) We wish I had the courage to fight back.

(3c) I wish that it were morning.

(3d) I wish I lived nearer London.

(3e) We never have enough time and we wish we had more.

(3f) I wish I could help you, but I can't.

(3g) I envy you. I wish I was going away too.

(3h) The woman wished she could help them.

(3i) He wished he had phoned for a taxi.

Grammar Tip 3 : 가정법(Subjunctive)

가정법이란 지금 이루지 못하거나 과거에 못했던 일을 아쉬워하거나, 현재 혹은 과거의 실제 사실과 반대되는 내용을 표현할 때 사용하는 독특한 어법(mood)으로, 영어를 포함한 서구어에서 폭 넓게 사용하며 영어에서는 일반 서술문과 구별하기 위해 문장의 '실제 시제보다 이전의 시제'라는 형식을 활용하여 표현한다.

A. 가정법과거

: 현재 사실의 반대, 이루어지지 않거나 이루지 못하는 일에 대해 아쉬워하거나 후회하는 마음을 표현할 때 사용되며 과거시제를 활용해서 일반 서술문과 구분되도록 한다. (원래'be–동사'의 경우 주어와 상관없이 'were'를 사용하나 종종 'was'가 사용되기도 한다.)

(1) If David was/were here, he would know what to do. (David isn't here and he can't know what to do.)

(2) If she could see him now, she'd be so proud. (She can't see him now.)

(3) If Jack was/were playing, they would probably win. (Jack can't play now, so we can't tell if they will win or not.)

B. 가정법 과거완료

: 과거 사실의 반대나 이루어 지지 않은 일에 대해 아쉬워했거나 후회했던 마음을 표현할 때 사용되며 과거완료시제를 활용해서 일반 서술문과 구분되도록 한다.

(4) I would have helped him if he had asked. (I didn't help him since he did not ask me.)

한편, 주절이나 종속절만 가정법을 사용하는 경우도 빈번하며 그 중 하나가 'I wish…'구문이다.

(5) I would have helped you, but you didn't ask me.

(6) You didn't ask me or I would have helped you.

(7) I wish I could help you, but I can't.

(8) He wished he had phoned for a taxi.

[4] wish + to-infinitive

(4a) I wish to be alone.

(4b) More people will wish to vote.

(4c) I wish to travel.

(4d) He said the West does not wish to advance NATO's forces beyond the present West German border.

[5] wish + Noun + to-infinitive

(5a) I wish it to be known that I disagree.

(5b) I wish you to come at three o'clock.

(5c) I wish him to come.

(5d) He wished me to attack and do the best I could with the troops available.

[6] wish + Noun + Adjective/-ing/-ed

(6a) She had no reason to wish him dead.

(6b) I wish him around.

(6c) I wish them ready for the new project.

(6d) We wish him well in his new post at the Amsterdam Hilton.

[7] wish + Noun + Noun

(7a) I wish you enormous courage.

(7b) I wish John Major all the luck in the world.

(7c) I wish them good luck.

(7d) He wished her good night.

(7e) I wish you a merry Christmas.

[8] Other Usage

(8) I would not wish such an illness on anyone.

영작문제 :

a. 그의 이름을 기억할 수 있으면 좋으련만. (기억 못하는 상태)

b. 나는 너를 다시 보기를 원한다.

c. 나는 네가 다시 오기를 바란다.

33. know

[1] know + ø

(1a) I don't know.

(1b) A: This pizza is great.

B: I know.

(1c) Please try to be, you know, a little quieter.

[2] know + Preposition(about, of)···

(2a) They knew about the risk they were going to take.

(2b) He knew about what was going on.

(2c) She knew of her husband's multiple affairs.

[3] know + Noun (+ Preposition···)

(3a) I know that face.

(3b) I don't know the answer to that question.

(3c) He knew a little Turkish.

(3d) I had known him for nine years.

(3e) I know a poem by heart.

(3f) A: The speed limit here is 35.

B: Yeah, I know it.

(3g) I really wanted to get to know America.

(3h) Do you know the difference between a degree and a diploma?

(3i) I knew her as a very happy, lovely person.

(3j) They all knew him by name.

(3k) The drug is commonly known as Ecstasy.

(3l) Peter Wilson is also known as 'the Tiger'.

[4] know + Nominal Clause

(4a) He knew that he was being followed.

(4b) I know she won't fail.

(4c) I'll find out about the car and let you know what's happened.

(4d) Do you know how he did that?

(4e) I knew that she had recently graduated from law school.

(4f) I should have known that something was seriously wrong. (In fact, I didn't know…)

[5] know + (wh−pronoun) + to−infinitive

(5a) I didn't know what to say to this.

(5b) I don't know where to go for the information.

(5c) No one knew how to repair it.

(5d) Do you know how to drive?

[6] know + Noun + to−infinitive

(6a) As for women, he knew them to be stronger and healthier than men.

(6b) A daily intake of 20mg of vitamin C is known to be sufficient in most cases.

(6c) He has been known to spend all morning in the bathroom.

[7] Other Usage

(7) By now the boys know right from wrong, but peer pressure is strong.

영작문제 :

a. 나는 그의 목소리를 안다.

b. 그녀는 음악에 대해 아무것도 몰랐다.

c. 나는 그녀의 남편에게 무슨 일이 일어났는지 모른다.

d. Joanna는 그의 아버지가 얼마나 지는 것을 싫어하는지(*hate to lose*) 알았다.

e. 나는 이 상황을 어떻게 대처해야(*deal with*) 할 지 모르겠다.

f. 무슨 말을 해야 할지 모르겠다. (할 말이 없다.)

g. Martin Scorcese는 미국의 가장 위대한 영화감독들 중 하나로 알려져 있다.

34. see

[1] see + ø

(1a) My father may be deaf, but he can see.

(1b) Let me see…, What was his name?

(1c) As you can see, life in medieval Europe was difficult.

[2] see + Noun

(2a) I missed everything – I didn't see a thing.

(2b) NATO sees the need to reform itself.

(2c) The decade saw a decline in living standards in much of Africa.

(2d) Fred Wright went to see Scott and find out how he keeps his birds.

(2e) I will be seeing her this week anyway.

(2f) See you later!

(2g) I see your point.

(2h) I can't see him as a president.

[3] (can) see + Nominal Clause

: 조동사 'can'과 함께 쓰일 때는 '알 수 있다'의 의미로도 쓰인다.

(3a) I saw that his eyes had reddened behind the thick glasses.

(3b) You could see he'd made his mind up.

(3c) I don't see why you should be ashamed.

(3d) You can see where you went wrong.

(3e) See who's at the door.

(3f) She could see that he was worried as well as puzzled.

(3g) I can see why they're worried.

(3h) I could see his point.

(3i) I can't (don't see) see why he is so upset.

[4] see + Preposition…

(4a) I must see about selling the house.

(4b) I'll see to that immediately as soon as I arrive at the office.

(4c) No man can see to the end of time.

(4d) We'll see about changing your dorm room later.

(4e) Please see after the children while I'm gone.

(4f) Will you please see Ms. Smith out?

(4g) We saw through his superficial charm.

[5] see + Noun + ø –Infinitive

(5a) She saw him fall flat on his back.

(5b) They saw her go out.

(5c) She was seen to go out.

(5d) As it took off, the biplane was seen to be in serious trouble.

[6] see + Noun + Adjective/–ing/–ed/Preposition…(Adjectival Phrase)

(6a) I hate to see you so unhappy.

(6b) One witness saw the youths running towards the main road.

(6c) I can't see him running the risk of taking on an uninsured worker.

(6d) I cannot stand by and see a child in pain.

(6e) Much of the ritual will be seen live on television.

(6f) He was seen going to various village stores, buying stuff.

(6g) The United States would like to broaden NATO's geographical horizons rather than see it supplanted by other organizations.

영작문제 :

a. 그 운동선수(*the athlete*)는 이번 주에 의사를 만나기를 원한다.

b. 그녀는 그가 집밖으로 나가는 것을 보았다.

c. 그 남자는 나가는 것이 보였다.

d. 그는 자신의 친형이 살해당하는(*murdered/killed*) 것을 보았다.

e. 우리는 그가 실수를 저질렀다는 것을 알 수 있었다.

f. Andrew는 2008년 6월 7일에 살아 있는 모습이 마지막으로 포착되었다. (그날 마지막으로 모습이 보였다.)

35. find

[1] find + Noun

(1a) I thought I'd find him here.

(1b) She asked advice about finding an apartment.

(1c) I could find another job for him.

(1d) I found a dime on the floor.

(1e) So what have they found about the changes in the Arctic and in the Antarctic?

[2] find + Nominal Clause

(2a) They searched the text to find where the answer is.

(2b) They found that the man was innocent.

(2c) I found that I couldn't do the work.

[3] find + Preposition(out)…/Adverb(out)

(3a) How did you find out?

(3b) I found out the phone number by looking it up.

(3c) They'll be sorry when they find out their mistake.

(3d) She was afraid her husband would find out about their relationship.

[4] find out + Nominal Clause

: 이 경우 'find out' 자체가 하나의 구동사로 쓰여 뒤에 문장이 온다.

(4a) This American agent found out that Stu knew about it.

(4b) Find out whether he is responsible for that or not.

(4c) They never found out how he escaped.

(4d) I found out what she was really like.

(4e) I found out what was troubling her.

(4f) I found out from his teacher that he hadn't been to school.

[5] find + Noun + Noun

: 목적어가 둘일 경우 '…에게 …을 찾아주다'의 의미로 사용된다.

(5a) We tried to find her a home.

(5b) I'm sure you'll find him a good worker.

[6] find + Noun + to-infinitive/-ing/-ed/Adjective/Preposition···
(Adjectival Phrase)

(6a) They found him guilty.

(6b) I found the British weather very cold.

(6c) Marks would find it hard to keep his job.

(6d) She found the new job difficult at first but she soon found her feet.

(6e) She returns from the bathroom to find him sitting on the floor.

(6f) I found his behaviour extremely rude.

(6g) Anderson found himself out of a job.

(6h) I find it ludicrous that nothing has been done to protect passengers from fire.

(6i) There was a young woman found dead in a local park.

영작문제 :

a. 우리는 그 개가 죽어가는 것을 발견했다.

b. 나는 그가 이미 죽은 사실을 알게 되었다.

c. 그녀는 다른 일자리를 얻기(*find another job*)가 힘들다는 것을 알게 될 것이다.

d. 그는 내게 저렴한(*inexpensive*) 차를 찾아주었다.

36. realize

[1] realize + Noun

(1a) You need to realize your full potential.

(1b) I realized the seriousness of the crime.

(1c) He finally realized his lifelong ambition to learn how to play the violin.

(1d) She realized a substantial return on the investment. ('실현하다'의 의미)

[2] realize + Nominal Clause

(2a) I realized something was wrong.

(2c) Do you realize that you are two hours late?

(2c) People don't realize how serious this recession has actually been.

(2d) As soon as I saw him, I realized that I'd seen him before.

(2e) I began to realize that it would be impossible.

영작문제 :

a. 그는 자신의 한계를 깨달아야한다.

b. 그들은 자신들이 위험에 처했다는 사실을 깨닫지 못했다.

37. let

[1] let + Noun + ø –Infinitive

(1a) Let me know what you find out.

(1b) She let him talk.

(1c) Let me think!

[2] let + us + ø −Infinitive

(2a) Let's have a sandwich.

(2b) Let us see what damage has been done.

(2c) Let us look at these views in more detail.

[3] let + Noun + Preposition…

(3a) I can let you into the secret, but we don't tell anyone else.

(3b) Just pretend to show me papers and I'll let you through.

(3c) I'd better go and let the dog out.

(3d) Let him in.

[4] Other Usage

(4) She let go of Mona's hand.

영작문제 :

a. 어제 무엇을 내가 보았는지 너에게 말해줄게.

b. 우리 이 문제를 해결해 보자.

c. 그를 들여보내.

38. force

[1] force + Noun (+ Preposition…)

(1a) I was gazing at him and he forced a smile.

(1b) I forced my foot into the shoe.

(1c) He forced his ideas upon the group.

(1d) They forced him into marrying her.

(1e) They forced me into signing the agreement.

(1f) The decision was forced on him.

[2] force + Noun + Adjective/to-infinitive

(2a) He tried to force the window open.

(2b) The rise of the Nazis forced the family to move to London.

(2c) He forced me to give him money.

(2d) People of my age group were forced to go to church.

(2e) He was forced to take a second job.

(2f) I am forced to admit that I was wrong.

(2g) I had to force myself to stay calm.

[3] Other Usage

(3) He forced out an apology.

영작문제 :

a. 그들은 그녀가 그 동의서에 사인하도록(*sign the agreement*) 강요하였다.

b. 그녀는 결국 그 결론에 이르도록(*to the conclusion*) 강요되었다.

c. 가난이 그가 죄를 짓도록(*commit crimes*) 만들었다.

d. 그는 그 그룹에(*upon the group*) 자신의 생각(*his ideas*)을 강요했다.

39. have

[1] have + Noun

(1a) I dream of having a fast car.

(1b) You had a tough time when you were little.

(1c) I have no money.

(1d) He had doubts about their loyalty.

(1e) I had a letter from my cousin.

(1f) I won't have that kind of behavior in my house.

(1g) Your opponent in the debate had you on every issue.

(1h) She is going to have a baby.

(1i) The children are having a party.

(1j) I was having a chat with an old friend.

[2] have + to-infinitive

(2a) It is hard on you having to cope with this twice.

(2b) Children have to have somewhere to play.

(2c) We simply have to get there on time.

[3] have + Noun + ø -Infinitive/Adjective/-ing/-ed

(3a) Mark had my assistant run the errand and I didn't like it.

(3b) I'll have Kim serve you breakfast in bed.

(3c) I'd never had people feel like that about me.

(3d) I'll have dinner ready.

(3e) Have you had your hair short then?

(3f) I had my car repaired.

(3g) We've just had the house decorated.

(3h) They had him killed.

(3i) The recall of a stunning half a billion eggs has some politicians saying that now is the time to toughen food safety laws.

[4] Other Usage

(4a) I've had it with your excuses.

(4b) Your ambition had a lot to do with your success.

(4c) She's got two sisters.

(4d) We haven't got a car.

(4e) have + Noun : have a good time, have a walk, have a look at, have a bath, have a headache, etc.

영작문제 :

a. 우리는 다시 시작해야 한다.

b. 나는 시계를 도둑맞았다.

c. 나는 비서에게 e-mail을 보내게 했다.

d. 나는 머리를 잘랐다. (커트 서비스를 받았다.)

40. allow

[1] allow + Noun (+ Preposition…)

(1a) They have allowed no such luxury to anyone else.

(1b) The schedule allows time for a coffee break.

(1c) No pets are allowed inside.

(1d) Running was not allowed in the school.

(1e) The schedule allows time for a coffee break.

(1f) Burma had not allowed foreign journalists and other observers into the country.

[2] allow + Noun + Noun

(2a) They allow a person $100 for expenses.

(2b) The teacher allowed them 5 minutes to answer.

(2c) Mandela was allowed few visitors in prison.

[3] allow + Noun + to-infinitive

(3a) He allowed me to take the course.

(3b) You must not allow a golden opportunity to slip through your fingers.

(3c) In 1986, I got joint custody of the children, but my wife has never allowed me to see them.

(3d) The public should be allowed to make their own decision.

(3e) Visitors are not allowed to take photographs in the museum.

[4] allow + Nominal Clause

(4a) I had to allow that he was right.
(4b) Mother allowed that we'd better come in for dinner.
(4c) I certainly would allow that things had taken an unfortunate turn.

[5] Other Usage

(5a) Gently pour the butter into the sieve and allow to drain through undisturbed.
(5b) The premise allows of only one conclusion.
(5c) Originally the scheme allowed for pensions to be calculated on the best twenty years of earnings.
(5d) Even allowing for the fact that in several sports the Americans didn't field their strongest teams, no one expected Cuba to do so well.

영작문제 :

a. 나는 네가 그렇게 행동하도록 허용할 수 없다.
b. 정부는 그들이 TV에 광고하는(*advertise on TV*) 것을 허락할 것이다.
c. 아이들은 폭력이 심한 (*violent*) TV 프로그램을 보지 못하도록 되어 있다.
d. 여기서 담배를 피우시면 안 됩니다.

41. admit

[1] admit + Noun

(1a) No one has admitted responsibility for the murder.

(1b) He admitted his guilt.

(1c) Each ticket admits two people and is valid until the end of October.

(1d) Six people were admitted to hospital with bullet wounds or injuries from bomb explosions.

(1e) Children under six are admitted free.

[2] admit + Nominal Clause

(2a) He admitted that he was wrong.

(2b) Philip admits he can't walk past a bookshop without going in.

(2c) I have to admit that I have bad handwriting, but that is not a moral fault of mine.

(2d) I had to admit, sir, there's one thing that worries me.

(2e) I am ashamed to admit what a relief this was.

(2f) I'm talking about the people who admitted to me they were guilty.

[3] Other Usage

(3a) So far no group has admitted carrying out the murder.

(3b) Your father did not admit to his blindness and your mother, long after his death, continued to behave as if he had not died.

(3c) Admittedly, she is not well.

영작문제 :

a. 그들은 뇌물을 받은(*take bribes*) 것을 시인했다.

b. 시험이 어려웠음을 인정한다.

42. ask

[1] ask + Preposition(for, about)…

(1a) He asked for help.

(1b) We asked for the bill.

(1c) He was reported to have asked for an extra one thousand million dollars.

(1d) She asked about obtaining a rule book.

(1e) She asked about God.

[2] ask + Noun(Direct Object or Indirect Object)

(2a) I've no idea. You must ask my wife.

(2b) She asked permission to leave the house.

(2c) When we realized that we didn't know the answer, we asked the teacher.

(2d) The job asks both time and patience.

[3] ask + Noun + Preposition(for, about, to, etc.)···

(3a) Elenor asked Frank for some money.

(3b) I asked her for dinner the following evening.

(3c) Leeds asked me to the trial.

(3d) I asked them for attention.

(3e) Jim asked them to dinner.

(3f) She asked him about God.

(3g) She asked ten dollars for the book.

[4] ask + Nominal Clause

(4a) Helen wrote home and asked if she could come for Christmas.

(4b) The US will ask that the Security Council meet in special session next Thursday.

(4c) A young man asked if we were students.

(4d) I asked whether they liked the film.

[5] ask + Noun + Noun

(5a) The police officer asked me a lot of questions.

(5b) Can I ask you a favor?

(5c) I was asked my opinion about the new car.

[6] ask + Noun + to-infinitive

(6a) She asked him to come with her.

(6b) He asked her to help him by going to the Island.

(6c) He asked her to marry him.

(6d) I asked him to help me.

[7] ask + Noun + Nominal Clause

(7a) She asked him if he spoke French.

(7b) I asked Brian whether he agreed.

(7c) Someone asked me if the work was going well.

(7d) When she asked him how he as feeling, he could not bring himself to speak.

(7e) I asked him what he wanted.

(7f) He asked me where I was going.

(7g) I asked him if he could help.

(7h) A Black girl was asked why she 'Talks White.'

[8] Other Usage

(8a) He asked me how to spell the word.

(8b) Don't be afraid to ask how to operate those new machines.

(8c) The church leaders mediating in the talks have asked to see President Momoh.

(8d) Should I ask her out?

영작문제 :

a. 우리는 그녀에게 어떻게 이 문제를 해결해야 할지 물었다.

b. 그들은 그가 집에 가게 허용되어야 한다고 나에게 요청했다.

c. 우리는 그들에게 떠나라고 요청했다.

d. 그들은 나에게 그 컴퓨터 값으로 $800을 내라고 요구했다.

e. 나는 그 컴퓨터 값으로 $800을 내라고 요구받았다.

f. 나는 그에게 열심히 일하라고 당부했다.

g. 그는 내게 세 가지 질문을 했다.

43. expect

[1] expect + Noun (+ Preposition…)

(1a) I am expecting a phone call.

(1b) We expect good news today.

(1c) Robin was expecting an important letter from France.

(1d) We expect an apology

(1e) My wife, Sarah, is expecting a baby in November.

(1f) We are expecting rain.

(1g) Rain is expected on Sunday.

(1h) A lot of people expect a lot from you just now.

(1i) He expected a reward for finding her the watch.

(1j) That has long been expected of prime ministers.

[2] expect + to-infinitive

(2a) He expects to win.

(2b) To tell you the truth, I wasn't expecting to hear from you again.

(2c) When can we expect to see any results?

(2d) I did not expect to be acknowledged.

[3] expect + Nominal Clause

(3a) I expect he had some strong reason.

(3b) I expect there's lots more to come.

(3c) I don't expect that it will be necessary.

(3d) I expect they've gone.

[4] expect + Noun + to-infinitive/Adverb

(4a) I expect him to come soon.

(4b) They expected me to succeed in this project.

(4c) They are expected to leave now.

(4d) She is expecting him back in the late afternoon.

(4e) The boss expects us to work late today.

(4f) The talks are expected to last two or three days.

[5] Other Usage

(5) Shearer's wife Leana is expecting.

영작문제 :

a. 오늘 밤 눈이 예상됩니다.

b. 나는 John에게서 소식을 곧 듣기를 예상한다.

c. 나는 네가 내 규칙을 따라주길 기대한다.

d. 아무도 네가 불가능한 것을 성취하리라고(*achieve the impossible*) 기대하지 않는다.

e. 나는 비행시간이 한 시간일 것으로 예상한다.

f. 그가 금요일에 올 것을 예상한다.

g. 회담(*talks*)이 내일까지 계속될 것이 예상됩니다.

44. help

[1] help + ø

(1a) I could cook your dinner if that would help.

(1b) He believes an extra layer of scrutiny by lawyers will help.

(1c) I made a cake, and my friend helped.

(1d) He has a bad back, and physical therapy hasn't helped.

(1e) Crying won't help.

(1f) Again this may help in obtaining a discount on the insurance premium.

(1g) Help! I am stuck!

[2] help + Noun (+ Preposition(with)⋯)

(2a) Can I help you, sir?

(2b) I was wondering if you might be able to help me.

(2c) She called me before the meeting because she said I was ready to help the group.

(2d) Can you help me with my homework?

(2e) She helped me with my project.

(2f) I know a win would certainly help my chances with the team.

(2g) Please help the customer in aisle 20.

[3] help + to-infinitive/ ø -infinitive

: 'help'는 종종 원형부정사와 함께 쓰인다.

(3a) B-complex vitamins help to neutralize chemical poisons in the body.

(3b) The project was brought in to help to rescue people in 1989.

(3c) I used to help cook the meals for the children.

(3d) The money helped pay the rent.

(3e) This policy helped to improve the competitiveness of American exports.

(3f) The taxi driver helped to carry the bags into the hotel.

(3g) You can help save the lives of dolphins.

(3h) The idea is to help create a better understanding between the police and the man and woman in the street.

(3i) She says it might have helped prevent the egg recall from getting so big.

[4] help + Noun + to–infinitive/ ø –infinitive

(4a) I helped her find her book.

(4b) The therapist deliberately does not help them to break through.

(4c) We must try to help students to have confidence in their ability.

(4d) He helped his friend to escape; she helped him climb out of the boat.

(4e) He's the one who can help England reach the World Cup finals.

(4f) The following exercise can help you distinguish between the two.

(4g) Something went wrong with his machine so I helped him fix it.

[5] cannot help + Gerund/Noun

(5a) I couldn't help laughing.

(5b) We can't help admiring her.

(5c) I couldn't help teasing him a little.

(5d) Maybe he can't help it.

[6] cannot (help) but + Infinitive

(6a) He couldn't help but go.

(6b) I couldn't help but tease him.

(6c) I cannot help but like him.

(cf.) a) People cannot but protest against injustice.

b) What could he do but forgive her?

c) Employees cannot choose but finish the given tasks.

[7] Other Usage

(7a) Help me off with these boots.

(7b) Help your grandmother on with her coat.

(7c) Help yourself to the cookies.

영작문제 :

a. 나를 도와줄 아무도 없었다.

b. 그녀는 서류 작성하는(*write the document*) 일을 도왔다.

c. 나는 그녀가 그 책을 쓰는 것을 도왔다.

c. 우리는 그를 존경할 수밖에 없다.

d. 제 리포트를 도와주시겠습니까?

e. 그것은 그 사건을 설명하는 데(*in explaining the incident*) 도움이 될 것이다.

45. require

[1] require + Noun

(1a) He requires a quiet hotel room when he travels.

(1b) Most plants require plenty of water.

(1c) The law requires full disclosure of charitable donations.

(1d) Skiing requires practice.

(1e) This work requires precision.

(1f) Your presence is urgently required.

(1g) I will do everything that is required of me.

(1h) An increase in funds may be required.

[2] require + Nominal Clause

: 동사의 의미에 '의무' 등을 포함하는 관계로 종속절에 'should' 조동사가 쓰이며 종종 생략되곤 한다.

(2a) Some firms require that memos (should) be one page or shorter.

(2b) The chairman required that all be silent.

(2c) The regulations require that all students should attend at least 90% of the lectures.

(2d) It is required that I should appear in court.

[3] require + Noun + to-infinitive

(3a) His responsibilities required him to visit other locations.

(3b) He requires the students to present their papers.

(3c) The school requires all students to study mathematics.

(3d) 'Truth in Menu' requires us to tell the truth about the things that we serve in our restaurants.

(3e) You are required to complete a special form.

(3f) The situation requires me to take immediate action.

(3g) You are required to report to the police.

(3h) All the boys were required to study religion.

[4] Other Usage

(4) Confidence in male prowess doesn't require talking big or even being big.

영작문제 :

a. 이 일은 경험을 요구한다.
b. 우리는 반드시 떠나라는 요구를 받았다.
c. 그 계약서(*contract*)는 우리가 그 일을 일주일 안에 끝내도록 요구한다.
d. 그 계약서에 따르면 우리는 그 일을 일주일 안에 끝내야만 한다.

46. suggest

[1] suggest + Noun (+ Preposition…)

(1a) Such a crime suggests apt punishment.
(1b) Laura first suggested this idea to me.
(1c) A medical report has suggested a link between childhood leukemia and exposure to radiation through working at Sellafield.
(1d) I have suggested you as being the man for the job.
(1e) Someone else had suggested me as the writer.
(1f) Someone had suggested it to him as an investment.
(1g) I suggest Smith for the post.
(1h) We have to suggest a list of possible topics for next term's seminars.

[2] suggest + Nominal Clause

: '…할 것을 제안하다'의 의미로 쓰일 때 종속절에 조동사 'should'가 쓰이거나 생략된다.

(2a) The police officer seemed to be suggesting that the death was not an accident.

(2b) He suggested that they should meet that afternoon.

(2c) It can be hard for doctors to suggest how you should manage your illness.

(2d) I suggest to you that we go to the cinema or something.

(2e) Evidence suggests that exposure to lead may cause mental damage.

(2f) It was suggested that he should go.

(2g) I suggest that he should write her a letter.

(2h) I'm not suggesting we leave her here.

(2i) He suggested she talk to a psychologist.

(2j) His wife suggested that he should start a school.

[3] suggest + V-ing

(3a) The Council members suggest appointing a task force to study the problem.

(3b) It is with reluctance that I suggest spending more on it.

[4] Other Usage

(4a) It really did suggest the mind gradually disintegrating.

(4b) You might get a good counsellor that might suggest you doing a college course or something.

(4c) The evidence suggests otherwise.

영작문제 :

a. 그는 새 절차(*new procedure*)를 위원회에 제안했다.

b. 나는 한국식당을 그 회의 장소로 제안했다.

c. 그녀는 우리가 그것을 계약서에 써 넣어야 한다고 제안했다.

d. 너는 내가 지금 거짓말을 하고 있다는 것이냐(*Are you suggesting*…)?

e. 나의 가정의(*family doctor*)는 내게 매일 산보하라고(해야 한다고) 제안한다.

f. 그의 태도는 그가 정말로 관심이 없다는 것을 암시한다.

g. 어디에서 내가 약국을 찾을 수 있는지 알려주겠니?

47. propose

[1] propose + Noun (+ Preposition(for)…)

(1a) British Airways has proposed a one-way surcharge of $57.

(1b) What do you propose?

(1c) His idea was first proposed in 1789.

(1d) I proposed my friend for the job.

(1e) He proposed a new plan for dealing with terrorism.

(1f) She proposed a new theory of relativity.

[2] propose + to-infinitive

: 아래의 문장 (2b)와 (2c)에서 보듯이 'to-부정사'의 부정의 의미가 전체 문장의 동사인 'propose'에 표현되어 있다. 이는 'want' 동사의 경우에도 마찬가지이다.

(2a) I propose to leave town now.

(2b) I do not propose to get deeply involved in it.

(2c) We do not propose to discuss this matter any further

(2d) I propose to focus attention on one type of resource.

(2e) He proposes to build a new house.

(2f) The senator proposed to abolish the sales tax.

(2g) What do you propose to do now?

(2h) I propose to focus attention on one type of resource.

[3] propose + V-ing

(3a) I propose writing her a letter

(3b) He proposed changing the name of the company.

(3c) How do you propose getting home?

(3d) So what do you propose doing now?

[4] propose + Nominal Clause

: '…할 것을 제안하다'의 의미로 쓰일 때 종속절에 조동사 'should'가 쓰이며 생략되기도 한다.

(4a) I propose that we go and see her.

(4b) They proposed that political strikes should be made illegal.

(4c) She proposed that the book (should) be banned.

(4d) It was proposed that the president be elected for a period of two years.

영작문제 :

a. 그는 논문에서(*in his paper*) 새 방법론(*a new methodology*)을 제안했다.

b. 그는 새 법안(*the new bill*)을 통과시킬(*pass*) 것을 제안한다.

c. 그는 우리가 새 법안을 통과시켜야 한다고 제안했다.

48. insist

[1] insist + Nominal Clause

: '…하여야 한다고 주장하다'의 의미로 쓰일 때 종속절에 조동사 'should'가 쓰이며 생략되기도 한다.

(1a) He insisted that I should go.

(1b) He insists he's a reformed character.

(1c) He insisted that his rights be respected.

(1d) He insisted that she was mad.

(1e) But airport officials insisted that passenger flights did leave the capital on schedule.

(1f) You must insist to those around you that change is what you want and need.

[2] insist + Preposition(on, upon)…

(2a) He insisted on his rights.

(2b) He insisted on her madness.

(2c) You can insist on seeing the manager.

(2d) He insists on punctuality.

(2e) She insisted on coming with me.

(2f) The Security Council is insisting on strict control over the sale of oil.

(2g) Akito always insists on sitting in the front seat of the car.

(2h) If the government do insist upon bringing this bill again before Parliament, there will be a great deal of controversy.

영작문제 :

a. 그는 철저한 조사(*thorough investigation*)를 주장했다.

b. 나는 그가 가야 한다고 주장했다.

c. 그는 복종(*obedience*)을 종용한다.

d. 그는 자기가 돈을 지불(*pay the bill*)하겠다고 주장했다.

49. cause

[1] cause + Noun

(1a) It is likely to cause some controversies.

(1b) Are you causing trouble again?

(1c) The bad weather is causing problems for many farmers.

(1d) The drug not only causes sleep and heavy tranquilization, they also causes amnesia.

(1e) Derive happiness from those things that don't cause pain to others

(1f) Changeable British weather conditions often cause major problems for sailors.

(1g) We are trying to find out what causes an earthquake.

[2] cause + Noun + Noun

(2a) Please don't cause us any more pain.

(2b) The project is still causing him a lot of problems.

(2c) It was a genuine mistake and it caused me some problems.

[3] cause + Noun + to-infinitive

(3a) The same situation can cause people to experience stress in a wide variety of ways.

(3b) A blow to the head had caused him to lose consciousness.

(3c) The poor harvest caused prices to rise sharply.

(3d) The experience had caused her to be distrustful of people.

(3e) A protein gets into animal cells and attacks other proteins, causing disease to spread.

영작문제 :

a. 그는 부모에게 많은 불행(*unhappiness*)을 끼쳤다.

b. 추운 날씨는 화초들(*plants*)을 죽게 했다.

c. 나의 잘못은 내게 많은 두통을 가져왔다.

50. plan

[1] plan + Noun

(1a) We plan a new park

(1b) Various ceremonies are planned for the occasion.

(1c) A meeting has been planned for early next year.

(1d) We're planning a trip to France in the spring.

[2] plan + Preposition(on, for)…

(2a) The organizers planned on a large crowd attending the event.

(2b) We hadn't planned on going anywhere this evening.

(2c) Many people don't plan for retirement and then find that they haven't saved enough money.

(2d) I plan on returning to London several days after Easter.

(2e) She plans on taking a break from acting to focus on her newly adopted daughter Edith.

[3] plan + to-infinitive

(3a) They plan to buy a house.

(3b) I planned to go to the wedding.

(3c) I am planning to visit him next week.

(3d) They plan to arrive some time after three.

[4] plan + Nominal Clause

(4a) They might plan where they would go.

(4b) They planned that the two routes would connect.

(4c) I've been planning how I'm going to spend the day.

(4d) It is planned that Angus will be moved to the Saint August hospital tomorrow.

[5] Other Usage

(5a) You must plan where to spend the dollars in order to spend them efficiently.

(5b) Elaine planned for him to return to her.

(5c) The economy this year is planned to grow five percent.

영작문제 :

a. 우리는 더 나은 교육체계를 계획하고 있다.

b. 그는 New York을 떠날 계획이다.

51. start

[1] start + ø (+ Preposition/Adverb…)

(1a) Once the fire starts, watch it carefully until the wood or coal begins to burn.

(1b) The prices start at $100.

(1c) They started for the summit.

(1d) The movie starts at nine.

(1e) The meeting started with a brief statement from the president.

(1f) He started as a factory worker.

(1g) Mr. Baker started off as an assistant to Mr. Steinberg.

(1h) He started out as a salesman.

(1i) The snowfall started at midnight.

(1j) The engines started with a roar.

(1k) We shall have to start out at dawn.

(1l) It's time we started off.

[2] start + Noun

(2a) She started the engine.

(2b) He started the car.

(2c) Now is probably a good time to start a business.

(2d) We start work at dawn.

(2e) It's just not enough money to start life over.

(2f) The manager started him in marketing.

[3] start + to-infinitive

(3a) Suddenly the thing started to spin in a circle.

(3b) She started to cry.

(3c) She started to dance.

(3d) Rafael started to run.

(3e) I started to feel the pressure.

[4] start + V-ing

(4a) The dog started barking.

(4b) He started laughing.

(4c) I'm too stubborn to start changing my behavior now.

(4d) She started cleaning the kitchen.

[5] Other Usage

(5a) He started poor.

(5b) The pianist started young.

(5c) It's a good age to start them getting interested in the world about them.

(5d) To start with, where and when did it happen?

영작문제 :

a. 나는 새로운 프로그램을 시작하려고 해.

b. 비가 오기 시작했다. (*It*…)

c. 그는 달아나기 시작했다.

d. 아버지는 14살 때 일을 시작하셨다.

e. 나는 조수(*an assistant*)로 출발했다.

f. 쇼는 7시에 시작한다.

52. begin

[1] begin + Ø (+ Preposition…)

(1a) The rain began around noon.

(1b) The play begins with a monologue.

(1c) Those shirts begin at $20.

(1d) The restaurant began as a ice–cream parlor.

(1e) The principal began as a math teacher.

(1f) It was hard to tell where the water ended and the beach began.

(1g) My career as a journalist was about to begin.

(1h) The course began with learning how to take off.

(1i) Could I begin with a few formalities?

[2] begin + Noun

(2a) It is not easy to begin this story.

(2b) Henderson began his life as a Texas oil man and he made piles of money.

(2c) We'll begin the meeting as soon as he arrives.

(2d) The teacher opened the book and began the lesson.

(2e) The company has begun research on a new product.

(2f) The US is prepared to begin talks immediately.

[3] begin + to-infinitive

(3a) She began to experience strong pain in her leg muscles.

(3b) The weight loss began to look more serious.

(3c) I began to e-mail you but got interrupted.

(3d) I was beginning to feel better.

(3e) Those measures do not even begin to address the problem.

[4] begin + V-ing

(4a) Snow began falling again.

(4b) We began talking about our experiences.

(4c) She had begun attending college to make a better life for her daughters.

[5] Other Usage

(5) To begin with, I'd like to know

영작문제 :

a. 그 이름은 C로 시작한다.

b. 그는 언론인(*a journalist*)으로서 그의 경력(*his career*)을 시작했다.

c. 그 문제는 지난 11월에 시작되었다.

d. 그는 어떻게(how to) 시작해야 할지 몰랐다.

e. 그들은 작은 사업(*small business*)으로부터 시작했다.

f. 그는 일어나서 움직이기 시작했다.

53. end

[1] end (+ Preposition…)

(1a) The meeting quickly ended.

(1b) The current agreement ends on November 24.

(1c) He ended with the question: “When will we learn?”

(1d) The concert ended with a Bach sonata.

(1e) I ended by saying that further instructions would be given to him later.

(1f) The letter ends by requesting a deadline.

(1g) The evening ended with a dramatic display of fireworks.

(1h) The incident could have ended in tragedy.

(1i) They ended by making themselves miserable.

[2] end + Noun

(2a) Let's end this discussion.

(2b) He wanted to end their friendship.

(2c) She began to weep. That ended our discussion.

(2d) The markets ended the week on a quiet note.

[3] end up + V–ing/Preposition(with, as, etc.)…

(3a) He ended up as an adviser to the president.

(3b) The painting ended up being sold for a million dollars.

(3c) You might end up getting something you don't want.

(3d) A lot of computer hardware ends up in landfill sites.

(3e) She was afraid to close the window and ended up with a cold.

(3f) We missed our train, and we ended up taking a taxi.

(3g) Every time they went dancing they ended up in a bad mood.

(3h) I thought my date was with Sally, but I ended up with her twin sister.

영작문제 :

a. 그는 그들과의 관계를 청산했다.

b. Mary는 결국 Tim과 남게/함께 있게 되었다.

c. 그는 결국 파산하게(*be bankrupt*) 되었다.

54. hear

[1] hear + Ø

(1a) Do you think he can hear?

(1b) Mary couldn't hear since it was so noisy there.

[2] hear + Noun

(2a) They refused to hear our side of the argument.

(2b) Didn't you hear the doorbell?

(2c) I hear you.

(2d) Can you hear me?

(2e) Can you hear the signal?

(2f) She heard no further sounds.

(2g) I could hear music in the distance.

[3] hear + Nominal Clause

(3a) I heard that she got married.

(3b) We often hear that people never really change.

(3c) I hear you want some company tonight.

(3d) Ann couldn't hear what he was saying.

(3e) You should hear how nasty you sound.

(3f) Did you hear what I said?

[4] hear + Preposition···

(4a) I heard about your accident.

(4b) I love to hear about people who do things like that.

(4c) We want to hear from you!

(4d) I don't want to hear about it.

(4e) Have you heard from him lately?

(4f) The police are anxious to hear from anyone who may know her.

(4g) I've never heard of such a thing!

(4h) I offered to pay but she wouldn't hear of it.

(4i) He wasn't heard of for a long time.

(4j) I have never heard of attracting badgers with peanut butter.

(4k) If you don't do your homework, you're going to hear from me.

[5] hear + + Noun + Ø−infinitive/−ing/−ed

(5a) I heard him open the door.

(5b) I heard you talking to her.

(5c) I heard Amy cry out in fright.

(5d) He heard Hajime shouting and laughing.

(5e) I could hear him crying.

(5f) Rachel heard him go to the sitting−room, but did not hear him close its door.

(5g) I heard the bells ringing

(5h) Every four years we hear the same comments made.

[6] Other Usage

(6a) We sometimes hear of people receiving the keys to the City of London.

(6b) I hear about you getting married

영작문제 :

a. 나는 한 외침(*a shout*)을 들었다.

b. 우리도 그것에 관해 당신으로부터 이야기를 듣고 싶습니다.

c. 무슨 일이 있었는지 들었어요?

d. 그가 한 말 들었니? (그가 뭐라고 말했는지 들었니)

e. 나는 그가 말하고(*speak*) 있는 것을 듣지 못했다.

55. listen

[1] listen + Ø

(1a) Sonia was not listening.

(1b) Listen, young lady. Don't you call me that!

(1c) I told you many times but you wouldn't listen.

[2] listen + Preposition(to, in)···

(2a) Children don't always listen to their parents.

(2b) He spent his time listening to the radio.

(2c) You need to listen to me this time.

(2d) Listen in tomorrow for the conclusion.

(2e) Someone was listening in on our call.

(2f) If she'd listened to me, she wouldn't have got into trouble.

영작문제 :

a. 이거 들어보세요.

b. 우리는 그에게 귀를 기울어 볼 필요가 있다.

56. remember

[1] remember + Ø

(1a) I can't tell you what happened, because I don't remember.

(1b) I don't remember and anyway it makes no difference.

(1c) Don't you remember about Anna?

[2] remember + Noun (+ Preposition…)

(2a) I'll try to remember the exact date.

(2b) I finally remembered the address.

(2c) He remembered the man well.

(2d) I can never remember phone numbers.

(2e) I remember things about her that I found very intelligent.

(2f) I remember her as pretty and sort of tallish.

(2g) You might remember him from the Polaroid commercials.

(2h) He's more remembered as being a young rebel.

(2i) She will be remembered for her wonderful sense of humor.

(2j) What do you remember about her voice?

[3] remember + Nominal Clause

(3a) I just remembered that it's your birthday today.

(3b) I don't remember what he looks like.

(3c) Do you remember where he lives?

(3d) I can remember where and when I bought each one.

(3e) I don't remember where I hid it.

(3f) I remember (that) you used to do the same.

[4] remember + to-infinitive

: 'to-부정사'와 함께 쓰일 경우 '앞으로 잊지 않고 …하다'는 의미를 갖는다.

(4a) Remember to buy some coffee at the store.

(4b) He remembered to turn the gas off.

(4c) Remember to call me tonight.

(4d) Did you remember to close the door?

(4e) You should remember to replace your child's toothbrush every three months or so.

[5] remember + V-ing

: 동명사와 함께 쓰일 경우 '과거에 있었던 행동이나 일을 기억 하다'의 의미를 갖는다.

(5a) I remember seeing you for the first time.

(5b) I remember asking one of my sons about this.

(5c) I can't remember ever talking to you at all.

(5d) I remember closing the door.

(5e) I remember watching the first men landing on the moon.

(5f) I remember sitting on bundles and suitcases, waiting for the train that would take us we didn't know where.

[6] Other Usage

(6a) I don't remember you asking me about that.

(6b) I remember her being a dominant figure.

(6c) I can't remember how to pronounce it.

영작문제 :

a. 나는 그의 친절함 때문에(*for his kindness*) 그를 기억한다.

b. William은 그의 너그러움으로(*for his generosity*) 기억될 것이다.

c. 6시에 전화하는 거 기억해(명심해).

d. 나는 그녀를 한번 만난 것을 기억한다.

e. 나는 오늘 밤 파티가 있다는(*we are having a party*) 사실을 기억한다.

f. 우리가 어디에 주차를 했는지 기억할 수 있니?

57. regret

[1] regret + Noun

(1a) I immediately regretted my decision.

(1b) I simply gave in to him, and I've regretted it ever since.

(1c) I very much regret the injuries he sustained.

(1d) London Transport regrets any inconvenience caused by these delays.

[2] regret + Nominal Clause

(2a) Ellis seemed to be regretting that he had asked the question.

(2b) They regretted that no real changes had occurred.

(2c) I regret that the United States has added its voice to such protests.

[3] regret + V-ing

: 이미 한 행동이나 벌어진 일에 대해 후회하는 의미를 갖는다.

(3a) Five years later she regrets having given up her home.

(3b) He bitterly regretted ever having mentioned it.

(3c) I regret not speaking to her before she left.

(3d) None of the women I spoke to regretted making this change.

[4] regret + to-infinitive

: '…하게 된 것이 유감스럽다'의 의미를 갖는다.

(4a) I regret to inform you that your application has not been successful.

(4b) I regret to inform you he died as a consequence of his injuries.

(4c) We regret to inform you that the remainder of 2016 has been cancelled.

영작문제 :

a. 나는 내가 한 말을(*what I said*) 후회한다.

b. 불편을 끼쳐 드렸다면(*any inconvenience*) 유감스럽게 생각합니다.

c. 유감스럽게도 시험에 떨어지셨음을 알려드립니다.

d. Jane은 돌아온 것을(돌아왔던 것을) 후회했다.

e. 저는 안타깝게도 당신의 친절한 초대를 받아들일(*accept your kind invitation*) 수가 없습니다.

58. look

[1] look + Ø

(1a) Look! Look here!

(1b) Wendy went outside to look.

(1c) If you look carefully, you can just see our house from here.

(1d) Don't look now, but there's someone staring at you!

[2] look + Adjective/Preposition···(Adjectival Phrase)

(2a) They looked strange.

(2b) You look very pale.

(2c) You don't look 15 years old.

(2d) The place looked a bit dirty.

(2e) The road looked straight and flat on the map

(2f) Nothing looks better with summer clothes than a tan.

(2g) The conference last week looked in jeopardy when some memebers refused to attend.

(2h) Manchester United are looking good for the championship.

[3] look + Preposition(Particle)/Adverb···

: 특별한 경우를 제외하고 불완전자동사로 쓰이기 때문에 'look' 동사는 전치사 혹은 부사와 함께 쓰여 목적어를 갖으며 다양한 의미로 사용된다.

(3a) Sometimes she looked at the old newspapers.

(3b) I looked for you everywhere.

(3c) I have looked at this kind of therapy in my chapters on healing.

(3d) One has to look on the bright side of things.

(3e) The Parliament also agreed to look into changing the country's constitution.

(3f) Can you look up the opening times on the website?

(3g) We need to look to ways of improving our marketing.

(3h) Who's going to look after the children while you're away?

(3i) Look for the applicants with the highest income.

(3j) He looked the painting over carefully.

(3k) Look out! There's a car coming.

(3l) They look like twins.

(3m) I don't know what I would look like now if I hadn't had the facelift.

(3n) What does it mean if a guy looks into your eyes deeply and then starts to cry?

(3o) Look out for special deals.

(3p) Looking to the future, we asked him what the prospects are for a vaccine to prevent infection in the first place.

(3q) Things are looking up in the computer industry.

(3r) I wasn't successful, so they looked down on me.

(3s) They look like stars to the naked eye.

(3t) What are the symptoms to look out for?

[4] look + as if/as though

(4a) She should always look as though she's having a terrific time.

(4b) By early 1982 it looked as if both governments were inching towards the idea of a treaty.

[5] Other Usage

(5a) He looks his age. She dressed up to look the part.

(5b) I'm not looking forward to it at all.

(5c) Let us look at how these decisions will be considered and taken.

(5d) We will look to whether we continue the name of Challenge or whether we change to a unique name that reflects our look.

(5e) It's not looking like he might go out and I wondered if you'd be interested.

(5f) We will look at how to enforce judgements later.

(5g) The European Community is looking to normalize relationships with Iran.

(5h) Can you look me in the eye and say that?

(5i) You should always look where you're going.

(5j) Look who's coming.

(5k) Look what happened to him.

(5l) Look what you've done now!

(5m) The house looks east.

(5n) The hotel looks out over the harbour.

(5o) So far it looks like Warner Brothers' gamble is paying off.

영작문제 :

a. 너 지금 슬퍼 보여.

b. 그는 우리를 쳐다보고는 미소를 지었다.

c. 그 책은 재미있을 것 같다.

d. 나는 아직도 직장을 찾고 있다.

e. 걱정 마. 내가 너를 돌봐 줄께.

f. 너 잠을 잘 못잔 것 같구나(*look*…*as if*…).

g. 그는 그의 형이랑 닮았다.

h. 나 어때 보여?

i. 그녀는 어떻게 생겼나요(*What*)?

59. discuss

[1] discuss + Noun

(1a) We discussed the matter briefly. (NOT, We discussed about the matter.)

(1b) She could not discuss his school work with him.

(1c) I am not prepared to discuss this on the phone.

(1d) The book discusses the challenges that journalists face today.

(1e) This topic will be discussed at greater length in the next chapter

[2] discuss + Nominal Clause

(2a) We need to discuss when we should go.

(2b) We discussed whether we should call the police.

(2c) We discussed who we should advocate.

[3] discuss + wh−pronoun + to−infinitive

(3a) We need to discuss what to do.

(3b) We discussed whether to call the police.

(3c) We discussed what to take.

[4] discuss + V−ing

(4) We briefly discussed buying a new car.

[5] Other Usage

(5) As we discussed yesterday, the problem could have more than one solution.

영작문제 :

a. 그 문제에 대해 누군가와 상의해 본 적 있니(*have you discussed*)?

b. 우리는 차를 한 대 더 살 것(*buy a second car*)에 대해 의논했다.

c. 우리는 기자회견을 할지(*hold a press conference*) 여부를 논의했다.

60. appear

[1] appear + Ø (+ Preposition…)

(1a) Grace had not appeared.

(1b) A plane suddenly appeared in the sky.

(1c) The first machines appeared during the 19th century.

(1d) Mr. Gorbachev appeared as a decent man in a decent suit.

(1e) He appeared at the party but left quickly.

(1f) he has appeared in many London productions.

(1g) He appeared in two plays.

(1h) The novel first appeared in installments in a magazine.

(1i) He has appeared in many London productions.

[2] appear + Adjective/−ed/−ing/Preposition···(Adjectival phrase)

(2a) He appeared even more relaxed than usual.

(2b) At present it appears impossible to prevent this.

(2c) She appeared surprised at the news.

(2d) The child appeared unhappy.

(2e) It appears promising.

(2f) He appears in good condition.

[3] appear + to−infinitive

(3a) He appears to be kind and simple.

(3b) They appear to have learned from their mistakes.

(3c) The aircraft appears to have crashed near Kathmandu.

(3d) Their offer appears to be the most attractive.

(3e) I appear to be misunderstood by everyone.

(3f) The evidence appears to support you.

(3g) They appear not to like each other.

(3h) She appeared not to notice.

[4] 'It appears' + Nominal Clause

(4a) It appears to me that you are right.

(4b) It appears you were correct after all.

(4c) It appears that I am misunderstood by everyone.

(4d) It appears that they will be late.

(4e) It appears you were correct after all.

[5] Other Usage

: 'seem' 동사의 'there seem to be' 구문과 마찬가지로 'appear'와 'there is' 구문이 혼합되어 'there appear to be'구문이 사용된다.

(5a) At present, there appears to be little prospect of their resumption in the near future.

(5b) There appears to be an error with the database.

영작문제 :

a. 그들은 결국 회의에 오지 않았다(나타나지 않았다).

b. 그는 그 상황을 알지 못하는(*unaware*) 것 같았다. (의식 못하는 것 같았다.)

c. 그들이 늦을 것 같다. (늦을 것처럼 보인다)

i) 주어가 they일 경우

ii) 주어가 it일 경우

61. watch

[1] watch + Ø

(1a) The men just watched and laughed.

(1b) Watch when you cross the street.

(1c) They just stood and watched while she carried all the bags inside.

[2] watch + Noun

(2a) All we need to do now is to sit back and watch the fireworks.

(2b) Watch your health.

(2c) Ella was scared that someone was watching her.

(2d) Watch your weight and take as much exercise as possible.

(2e) Watch his tongue.

(2f) Please watch your step.

(2g) We are being watched.

(2h) We watched the sunset.

(2i) He watched a tennis match on television.

[3] watch + Noun + −ing/−ed

(3a) She watched the kids playing in the yard.

(3b) Chris watched him sipping his brandy.

(3c) I watched the gulls hovering overhead.

(3d) The United States would continue to watch events unfold but would not interfere.

[4] Other Usage

(4a) Watch out!

(4b) He watched me clean the gun.

(4c) Just watch him run!

(4d) They watched the bus disappear into the distance.

(4e) He watched for signs of activity in the house.

(4f) If you can spare the time, spend a day watching how the light changes in strength and direction.

영작문제 :

a. 그 초병(*sentry*)은 밤새 경계를 했다/경계 근무를 섰다.

b. 그는 하루 종일 스포츠경기 중계를(*games on TV*) 시청했다.

c. 나는 그가 호텔로 들어가는/들어가고 있는 것을 목격했다.

62. cost

[1] cost + Noun

(1a) That camera cost $200.

(1b) Carelessness costs lives.

(1c) It cost $100 to put that one right.

(1d) It costs more to live in the city.

(1e) The wrong decision cost them dearly in the election.

(1f) It's going to cost us, Mr. President.

[2] cost + Noun + Noun

(2a) The accident cost her a broken leg.

(2b) The party corruption had cost two Soviet investigators their jobs.

(2c) That request will cost us two weeks' extra work.

(2d) Participating in the strike cost me my job.

영작문제 :

a. 숙식(*for lodgings and food*)으로 우리는 약 $300을 사용했다.

b. 그것은 그에게서 생명을 앗아갈 수도 있다.

c. 그의 부주의함이 그에게 직업을 잃게 했다.

d. 그 집은 그에게 돈이 많이 들었다. (그는 집에 많은 돈을 들였다.)

63. owe

[1] owe + Noun (+ Preposition(for, to)…)

(1a) He owed $2000.

(1b) I'll owe it to you.

(1c) I owe you for what you did.

(1d) I owe a great deal to him.

(1e) He owes his success to chance.

(1f) He owes his talent to his mother

(1g) We owe the plumber for services rendered.

(1h) He claims he is still owed for the work.

[2] owe + Noun + Noun

(2a) I don't owe him a penny.

(2b) You seem to owe your neighbors a grudge.

(2c) Now more and more I see I owe her everything.

(2d) I think I owe you an explanation.

(2e) We all owe him a drink for getting rid of that woman.

(2f) I owe him a lot for helping me to come back.

[3] Other Usage

(3a) He still owes for his house.

(3b) She still owes for the car.

영작문제 :

a. 그는 나에게 300달러를 빚지고 있다.

b. 너는 내게 사과를(*an apology*) 해야 한다.

c. 그는 운이 좋아서(*to good fortune*) 성공(*his success*)할 수 있었다.

64. send

[1] send + Noun (+ Adverb/Preposition…)

(1a) Who sent you?

(1b) The studio had to send a taxi for her.

(1c) I sent a copy to the office.

(1d) President might send American troops into combat.

(1e) The lion sent a roar through the jungle.

(1f) Russia sent troops into the Middle East.

(1g) The batter sent the ball to left field.

(1h) That music really sends me.

(1i) I always re–read my e–mails before I send them.

(1j) He had sent some flowers to Elena.

(1k) They sent me for an X–ray.

(1l) It has sent prices through the roof.

(1m) My attempt sent him into fits of laughter.

(1n) His lessons used to send me to sleep.

(1o) I ordered the servants to send him away.

(1p) I was sent away to boarding school at 13.

(1q) Please don't send me away again.

(1r) Please send him in.

(1s) The slight back and forth motion sent a pounding surge of pain into his skull.

[2] send + Noun + Noun

(2a) We can easily send you more details, if you want them.

(2b) Send us another doctor.

(2c) Myra sent me a note thanking me for dinner.

(2d) They send me a card every year for my birthday.

(2e) I sent you a text. Didn't you get it?

[3] send + Noun + –ing/Adjective

(3a) She sent him crashing to the floor.

(3b) The punch sent the fighter reeling.

(3c) Their music sent the fans wild.

(3d) The slap on my back sent me staggering.

(3e) A blow to the table sent the dishes flying.

(3f) All three major radio networks sent Roosevelt's speech live to home across America.

[4] Other Usage

(4a) Let's send in a letter of protest.

(4b) The coach is sending in the kicker.

영작문제 :

a. 그녀는 아들을 주립대학(*a State University*)에 보냈다.

b. 그 폭발은 유리잔을 날아가게 했다.

c. 내게 팩스를 보내주세요.

65. show

[1] show + Ø

(1a) He was very upset, but he didn't show.

(1b) A: Does my slip show?

B: It doesn't show.

(1c) Several designers are showing now.

(1d) Traces of snow and ice showed on the pavements.

(1e) The movie is now showing at all major movie theaters.

[2] show + Noun (+ Preposition…)

(2a) Figure 4.1 shows the respiratory system.

(2b) Here's a company that hasn't shown a profit since 1986.

(2c) She showed no interest in her children.

(2d) They showed displeasure at his remark.

(2e) Your work shows promise.

(2f) The film was first shown in 1968

(2g) I was shown into a large hall.

(2h) The picture shows him as a man in his thirties with a receding hairline.

[3] show + Nominal Clause

(3a) Evidence shows that the earth moves round the sun.

(3b) Research shows that a high-fiber diet may protect you from bowel cancer.

(3c) Research shows that doctors are working harder.

(3d) Opinion polls show that as much as 86 percent of the American public supports Mr. Bush.

[4] show + Noun + Noun

(4a) Have I shown you my hat?

(4b) He showed me his new car.

(4c) Show me some money.

(4d) He showed me his tatoo.

(4e) I showed them the city's historical sites.

(4f) They showed their parents no respect.

[5] show + Noun + Nominal Clause

(5a) She didn't want to show me how sad she was.

(5b) Show me which one you like and I'll buy it for you.

(5c) I showed them that I could do it.

(5d) Market research has shown us that people want quality, not just low prices.

[6] show + Noun + to-infinitive/Adjective

(6a) His new book shows him to be a first-rate storyteller.

(6b) He has shown himself to be ready to make compromises.

(6c) She had shown herself unable to deal with money.

[7] Other Usage

(7a) Ellen showed her how to apply it so that it lasts through the day.

(7b) Florist Juliet Willis will show how to make a Christmas ring for a table.

(7c) Young parents tend to show off their babies.

(7d) He showed off his new sports car.

(7e) She didn't show up.

(7f) Who is going to show us round?

영작문제 :

a. 그녀는 자신의 그림을 내게 보여주었다.

b. 그 보고서(*report*)는 우리가 건강보험개혁(*health care reform*)을 할 필요가 있음을 보여준다.

c. 그 보고서(*report*)는 국민들에게 건강보험개혁(*health care reform*)을 할 필요가 있음을 보여준다.

d. 내게 어떤 책을 네가 골랐는지 보여주렴.

e. 그 결과는 그가 전문가임을(*an expert*) 보여준다.

66. mean

[1] mean + Noun (+ Preposition…)

(1a) She meant so much to me.

(1b) The opinions of the critics meant nothing to him.

(1c) Magda didn't mean any harm.

(1d) Those dark clouds mean rain.

(1e) What do you mean by "perfect?"

[2] mean + to-infinitive

(2a) She didn't mean to hurt him.

(2b) I meant to go running this morning, but I overslept.

(2c) She didn't mean to hurt it.

(2d) If we had meant to stage a protest, we could have done a better job than that.

[3] mean + V-ing

(3a) Healthy living means being physically and mentally healthy.

(3b) I've got to do the right thing, even if it means taking a risk.

(3c) I had been a serious smoker and it meant giving up a 30-year, 35-a-day habit.

[4] mean + Nominal Clause

(4a) I thought you meant that you wanted some more to eat.

(4b) Did he mean (that) he was dissatisfied with our service?

(4c) If your child's flushed and feverish it could mean he's ill or simply that he's too hot.

(4d) The word "Limited" means that the owners of the company are only liable for the debts of the company up to the value of their share investment.

[5] mean + Noun + to-infinitive

(5a) I didn't mean her to read my letter.
(5b) I didn't mean it to sound like that.

[6] Other Usage

(6a) So what happens now? With your job, I mean.
(6b) I don't want to go. I mean, I want to, but I can't.
(6c) You're meant to pay before you go in.
(6d) I was never meant for the army.
(6e) Philip and Kim were meant for each other.

영작문제 :

a. 그것은 그녀에게 아무 의미도 없었다. (아무 것도 의미하지 않았다.)
b. 그 경기에서 이기는 것(*win this game*)은 내게 큰 의미가 있을 것이다.
c. 그런 말을 하는(*by saying that*) 의도가 무엇인가?
d. 그녀는 이 결혼을 원하지 않는다는 것을 의미(의도)한다(*She means*…).
e. 나는 네가 그것을 하라고(할 것을) 의미한 것이 아니었다.

67. believe

[1] believe (+ Adverb)

(1a) I believe so.

(1b) I believe not.

(1c) I don't believe so.

(1d) The good there believe and the bad disbelieve. (= believe in God)

(1e) Until someone can prove the film isn't genuine, there is no reason to believe otherwise.

[2] believe + Noun

(2a) I believe you.

(2b) Believe it or not, she bought it.

(2c) I can't believe that story.

(2d) Can you believe it? Five o'clock in the morning!

[3] believe + Preposition(in)···

(3a) We believe in free speech.

(3b) We believe in prevention rather than cure.

(3c) I believe in keeping the planet clean.

(3d) I believe in your ability to solve the problem.

[4] believe + Nominal Clause

(4a) I believe they will arrive shortly.

(4b) I believe God exists.

(4c) I believe they are out of town.

(4d) Police believe that the fire was started deliberately.

(4e) He really believed that there was something wrong with this man.

(4f) I couldn't believe how steep it was.

(4g) I just don't believe that Alan had anything to do with it.

(4h) She is, I believe, on her way here now.

(4i) It is believed that the couple have left the country.

(4j) It is believed that two prisoners have escaped.

[5] believe + Noun + to-infinitive/Adjective

(5a) She believed her son to be still alive.

(5b) We believe them to be hidden here in this apartment.

(5c) This is widely believed to be the tallest tree in England.

(5d) The vases are believed to be worth over $20000 each.

(5e) The bomb, (which was) believed to have been concealed in a truck, exploded in the morning in a commercial zone of Paris.

(5f) I wouldn't have believed it possible.

Grammar Tip 4 : 'Believe-동사'의 특별한 용례

A. 'Believe' 동사는 진행형으로 쓰이지 않는다. 가령 'I am believing you'라고는 표현하지 않으며 대신 'I believe you'라고 표현한다.

(1a) I believe that these findings should be presented to your readers.

(1b) (X) I am believing that these findings should be presented to your readers.

B. 'don't believe' 구문 :

'believe' 동사는 종속절에 부정을 사용하지 않고 주절인 'believe'에 부정을 표시한다. 즉 'believe that it is not true'라고 표현하지 않고 'don't believe that it is true'로 표현한다. 즉 아래의 (2a)와 (3a) 문장들은 의미상으로는 (2b)와 (3b)로 해석될 수 있으나 문장형식에 있어서 (2a)와 (3a)로 쓰인다.

(2a) I don't believe that Alan had anything to do with it.

(2b) (X) I believe that Alan did not have anything to do with it.

(3a) John doesn't think that he is competent.

(3b) (X) John thinks that he is not competent.

유사한 유형의 다른 동사들로는 'think, suppose' 등이 있다.

C. 의문사의 위치 :

'believe' 동사가 복합절을 구성하여 의문절이 목적어로 쓰일 때에는 (4)~(6)의 예문에서 보듯이 종속절의 의문사가 종속절 앞이 아닌 전체문장의 앞에 오게 된다.

(4) Who do you believe likes this book?

(5) How do you believe (that) I selected the article?

(6) Which article did you believe (that) I selected?

단 주절에 부정이 올 경우 의문사가 문장 앞으로 올 수 없다.

(7) (X) How don't you believe (that) I selected the article?

D. 수동 구문 :

본문 [4]의 (4i)와 (4j)의 문장들처럼 'believe' 동사의 목적어로 절이 오는 복합절이 수동형으로 쓰일 경우, 주어가 지나치게 길어지는 것을 피하기 위하여 가주어 'it'이 쓰인다. 즉 'They believe that two prisoners have escaped.' 문장은 'It is believed that two prisoners have escaped.'의 수동태가 된다. 그리고 이 문장은 다시 'Two prisoners are believed to have escaped'로 표현될 수 있다.

(8a) It is believed that the building is 700 years old.

(8b) The building is believed to be 700 years old.

(9a) It is widely believed that this is the tallest tree in England.

(9b) This is widely believed to be the tallest tree in England.

위의 (8b)와 (9b) 문장들은 각각 (8a)와 (9a)에서 유래했다고 볼 수 있으며 동시에 아래의 (10)과 (11)번 문장의 수동태 문장으로도 볼 수 있다.

(10) We believe the building to be 700 years old.

(11) They believe this to be the tallest tree in England.

영작문제 :

a. 코치는 우리가 그 경기를 이길 수 있다고 믿는다.

b. 나는 그가 무죄라고(*be innocent*) 믿는다.

c. 우리는 표현의 자유(*free speech/freedom of speech*)를 믿는다.

68. think

[1] think (+ Adverb)

(1a) A: That's how it would work. Don't you think so?

B: I think not. (I don't think so.)

(1b) She thought a bit before beginning an argument.

(1c) The referee has to think the way the players do.

[2] think + Noun

(2a) I can't think why.

(2b) A: This is our new company stationery. What do you think?

B: Stunning. Simply stunning.

A: We're considering moving out into the country. What do you think?

B: Sounds good to me.

(2c) It's no good thinking negative thoughts about other people.

(2d) That's what I was thinking.

[3] [think + Preposition(of, about, like)…] (+ Preposition(as)…)

(3a) They are thinking about moving.

(3b) I can't really think of a way round it, you know.

(3c) You were probably brought up to think like that.

(3d) What do you think of my theory?

(3e) But what do you think of it as a book?

(3f) I can't think of any reason why he should do that.

(3g) I just can't think of his name.

(3h) Many people think of angels as (being) benign, pleasant and helping.

(3i) She thinks of herself as a poet.

(3j) I was thinking of leaving home.

(3k) In China bats are thought of as being very lucky. (⇐ In China they think of bats as being very lucky.)

[4] think + Nominal Clause

: 아래의 Grammar Tip 5에서 보듯이 'believe' 동사와 마찬가지로 종속절의 부정사가 주절 동사인 'think'에 표시된다. 그리고 종속절의 의문사 또한 주절 앞에 위치하게 된다.

(4a) I think that's a good point.

(4b) I don't think that is entirely true. (NOT, I think that is not entirely true.)

(4c) I was thinking how awful it must have been.

(4d) Do you think I have to seal the boxes up?

(4e) It is thought that the storm is responsible for as many as four deaths.

(4f) Where do you think you're going?

(4g) Who do you think you're kidding?

(4h) Who do you think she is?

(4i) What do you think can make you a good tennis player?

[5] think + Noun + Adjective/-ing/-ed

(5a) I thought him charming.
(5b) She thought him blinded by love.
(5c) Nobody had thought him capable of that kind of thing.
(5d) They think my ideas impractical.

[6] [think + Preposition] + Nominal Clause
: 'think'와 전치사(불변화사)가 하나의 구동사로 간주되어 뒤에 절이 오기도 한다.

(6a) He thought of how he had met her.
(6b) What do you think about what's happening in Eastern Europe at the moment?
(6c) Next time you have a problem, think about how you can improve the situation instead of dwelling on all the negative aspects.

[7] think + to-infinitive
: '예상하다(expect)'의 의미로 'to-부정사'와 같이 쓰인다.

(7a) I didn't think to see you here.
(7b) I did not think to call you.

[8] Other Usage

(8a) People at the club think very highly of him

(8b) To tell the truth, I don't think much of psychiatrists.

(8c) I was thinking what to do.

Grammar Tip 5 : 'Think-동사'의 특별한 용례

A. 의문사가 오는 의문문

: 'think' 동사는 의문사와 함께 쓰일 때 타동사의 역할을 한다. 즉 'how'가 아닌 'what'와 함께 쓰인다.

(1a) What do you think about Korea?

(1b) (X) How do you think about Korea?

(2) How do you feel about Korea?

B. 수동 구문

: 아래 (3a)번처럼 복합절이 수동태로 쓰일 때 (3b) 문장처럼 종속절의 주어가 전체 문장의 주어로 올라가 쓰일 수 있으며 이 때 앞서 논의된 'say, believe' 동사들처럼 'to-부정사'가 쓰인다.

(3a) It is thought that the storm is responsible for as many as four deaths.

(3b) The storm is thought to be responsible for as many as four deaths.

즉 (4a) 문장은 (4b) 혹은 (4c)의 수동태 문장으로 쓰인다.

(4a) They think that the agreement includes the safe release of all the hostages.

(4b) It is thought that the agreement includes the safe release of all the hostages.

(4c) The agreement is thought to include the safe release of all the hostages.

C. 'don't think' 구문

: 'believe' 동사와 마찬가지로 종속절의 부정이 주절 동사인 'think'에 위치하게 된다. 아래의 (5)번 예들과 'guess' 동사가 주절에 오는 예문 (6)은 그 차이를 보여준다.

(5a) I don't think she is interested. (그녀가 관심이 없는 것 같다)

(5b) (X) I think she is not interested. ((5a)와 같은 의미로 쓰였을 경우)

(6a) I guess he is not interested. (그가 관심이 없는 것으로 추측된다.)

(6b) (X) I don't guess he is interested. ((6a)와 같은 의미로 쓰였을 경우)

D. 의문사의 위치

: 앞서 설명된 'believe' 동사의 경우처럼 의문절이 'think' 동사의 목적어로 쓰일 때 종속절의 의문사가 종속절 앞이 아닌 전체문장의 앞에 오게 된다. 즉 본문 [4]에 제시된 문장들 (4f)~(4i)는 다음과 같이 쓰일 수 없다.

(7a) (X) Do you think where you're going?

(4f: Where do you think you're going?)

(7b) (X) Do you think who you are kidding?

(4g: Who do you think you're kidding?)

(7c) (X) Do you think who she is?

(4h: Who do you think she is?)

(7d) (X) Do you think what can make you a good tennis player?

(4i: What do you think can make you a good tennis player?)

이는 다음 (8a)~(8d) 문장들에서의 'know' 동사와 비교된다.

(8a) Do you know where you're going?

(8b) Do you know who you are kidding?

(8c) Do you know who she is?

(8d) Do you know what can make you a good tennis player?

영작문제 :

a. 나는 그녀의 이름을 생각해내지 못했다.

b. 우리가 무엇을 할 수 있을지 생각해 보자.

c. 나는 이 문제에 대해 종종 생각해 왔다.

d. 우리는 그를 아버지처럼 생각해 왔다.

e. 그는 그 계약에서 빠져나갈(*get out of*) 다른 방법을 생각했다.

f. 어느 누구도 그런 기발한 software를(*such a clever piece of software*) 생각해 낸 사람이 없었다.

g. 나는 담배광고(*tobacco advertising*)를 금지해야(*ban*) 한다고 생각한다.

h. 네가 어디로 가고 있다고 생각하지?

i. 우리 새 계획이 잘 될까(*Will our new plan work*)?
아니, 그럴 것 같지 않아. (우리 계획이 제대로 작동할 것 같지 않다/작동할 거라고 생각하지 않는다.)

69. guess

[1] guess + Ø

(1a) First of all, I'm just guessing.

(1b) A: Can you find some information for me?
B: I guess so.

(1c) A: So no one actually saw him arriving?
B: No, I guess not.

(1d) You'll never guess.

[2] guess + Preposition…

(2a) We can only guess at her reasons for leaving.

(2b) We could only guess at his motives.

[3] guess + Noun

(3a) I guessed the answer.

(3b) He guessed my age.

(3c) He guessed the man's status from his appearance.

[4] guess + Nominal Clause

(4a) I guess he was wrong.

(4b) I guess he wanted you to know that.

(4c) You'll never guess what happened.

(4d) I guess I can manage alone.

(4e) I guessed what was going to happen at the end of the film.

(4f) Can you guess what we're having for dinner?

(4g) I guess he is not interested.

[5] Other Usage

(5a) I cannot guess what to do next.

(5b) I guess his age to be 50.

영작문제 :

a. 나는 그의 나이를 추측했다.

b. 그는 가격이 약 $500일거라고 추측했다.

c. 저 남자가 누구인지 추측할 수 있겠니?

d. 나는 그 도서관이 40만 권의 책을 보유할(*contain*) 것이라 추측한다.

70. suppose

[1] suppose + Ø

(1a) A: Shall we go?

B: I suppose so.

(1b) A: It doesn't often happen.

B: No, I suppose not.

(1c) A: You don't want this, do you?

B: I suppose not.

[2] suppose + Nominal Clause

: 'think, believe'와 마찬가지로 종속절의 부정 대신 주절에 부정이 오며 종속절의 의문사 또한 주절의 앞에 위치한다.

(2a) I suppose that it's too late to apply for the job now.

(2b) I suppose I was a bit rude.

(2c) Scientists supposed that large dinosaurs lived in swamps.

(2d) I don't suppose you'd like to come over and keep an old company? (NOT, I suppose you would not like to come over and keep an old company?)

(2e) I suppose he meant to kill her.

(2f) I don't suppose anyone cares much whether he stays or goes.

(2g) What do you suppose he will do? (NOT, Do you suppose what he will do?)

(2h) I don't suppose you've ever seen anything like this before!

(2i) I don't suppose you'd like to come out for a drink?

[3] Suppose, Supposing (that)…

(3a) Suppose we win the lottery.

(3b) Suppose you had a million dollars, what would you do?

(3c) Suppose we don't tell anyone, and somebody finds out about it.

(3d) Supposing something should go wrong, what would you do then?

(3e) Supposing he's right, it could be very serious.

[4] be supposed to… (suppose + Noun + to-infinitive)

: 'be supposed to…' 구문은 [suppose + Noun + to-infinitive] 구문 혹은 [suppose + Nominal clause] 구문의 수동태이며 일상적으로 자주 사용되는 표현이다.

(4a) I never supposed him (to be) a novelist.

(4b) The new laws are supposed to prevent the crime.

(4c) This machine is not supposed to make noise.

(4d) You are supposed to report it to the police as soon as possible.

(4e) I'm not supposed to talk to you about this.

영작문제 :

a. 비가 올 것 같다(*I suppose*…).

b. 그는 오늘 올 것으로 추정된다.

c. 그가 무죄라고 가정하자.

d. 만약 그녀가 그를 죽이지 않았다면 도대체 누가(*who on earth*) 그를 죽였을까?

e. 그녀는 여기서 나를 만나기로 되어 있었다.

Grammar Tip 6 : 'Believe so'와 'Believe not'

지금까지 본문에 제시된 동사들 중, 'believe, guess, hope, suppose, think' 등의 동사들은 목적절 혹은 앞서 제시된 문장의 내용에 대해 되풀이하거나 답할 때 긍정의 의미일 경우 동사 뒤에 'so'를 사용하여 간략하게 표현한다. 한편 부정의 의미일 경우에는 'guess, hope, suppose' 동사들은 간단히 동사 뒤에 'not'을 사용하는 반면 'believe'와 'think' 동사들은 일반적인 부정형을 사용하여 'don't believe so, don't think so' 등으로 표현한다. 그러나 간혹 (4)의 문장처럼 '동사+not'가 쓰이기도 한다.

(1) Chris thinks the tickets are too expensive, and Amy thinks so, too.

(2) A: Do you think the weather's going to be fine tomorrow?
B: I hope so. I want to do some work in the garden. (I hope the weather's going to be fine.)

(3) They asked Thelma if she thought her mother would refuse the invitation. She said she didn't think so.

(4) Are we prepared to change our entire lives for the sake of one person? I think not.

(5) A: It looks as if Lynda won't be coming with us after all.

B: I guess not. It's a pity.

(6) She thinks she might lose her job in the New Year, but she hopes not.

(7) A: Did Frances come here this morning?

B: I don't believe so, Ask Hannah.

이외에 'appear, be afraid('유감이다'의 의미), presume, seem' 등의 동사들도 동사 뒤에 'so'를 써서 간략하게 표현한다. 특히 'be afraid' 는 부정의 경우 'not'와 함께 쓰인다.

(8) A: Are you working on Saturday?

B: I'm afraid so, I wish I wasn't! (I'm afraid I'm working.)

(9) A: Can we speak to Mr. Baker, please?

B: I'm afraid not. He's busy. (I'm afraid you cannot speak to Mr. Baker.)

71. suspect

[1] suspect + Noun

: 목적어나 목적어로 쓰인 종속절의 의미를 부정하는 'doubt'와 달리 'suspect'는 다양한 의미로 쓰인다. 즉 'suspect'는 (1a)와 (1b)의 문장에서는 '의심하다'의 의미로 쓰이는 반면 (1c)에서는 '확신은 없으나 …한 것으로 추정(의심)한다'는 의미로 쓰인다.

(1a) I suspect his motives.

(1b) She suspected his sincerity.

(1c) If you suspect a gas leak, do not strike a match or even turn on an electric light.

[2] suspect + Nominal Clause

: 특히 명사절 목적어의 경우, 뒤의 내용을 의심하기보다 확신은 없으나 그럴 것으로 추정한다는 의미로 자주 쓰인다.

(2a) She suspects that he enjoyed having her with him.

(2b) I suspect that he is allergic to cats.

(2c) I suspect they were right.

(2d) If you know or suspect that a child is being ill-treated or neglected, please tell the NSPCC at once.

[3] suspect + Noun + Preposition(of)···

(3a) They had no reason to suspect him of anything.

(3b) I suspect him of giving false evidence.

(3c) The teacher suspected him of cheating.

(3d) I suspect him of killing the girl

(3e) He is suspected of being a spy.

(3f) He was suspected of terrorism.

(3g) He resigned after being suspected of theft.

[4] suspect + Noun + to-infinitive

(4a) Wendy suspected the man to be the murderer.

(4b) At first, various authorities suspected it to be simply a freak, extra-limited individual of some already-known species.

(4c) He is suspected to have started the fire.

[5] Other Usage (with the adjective form)

(5) I'm always suspicious of men like him.

영작문제 :

a. 나는 그가 술을 마신 것으로 생각했다.

b. 나는 Dan이 우리에게 거짓말을 한 것으로 생각한다.

c. 경찰은 살인혐의로 그를 의심하고 있다.

d. 그는 살인혐의를 받고 있다.

e. 그는 테러로 혐의를 받고 있었다.

72. doubt

[1] doubt + Noun

(1a) He doubted their motives.

(1b) A: Do your family know you're here?

B: I doubt it.

(1c) I never doubted you.

(1d) He might have a screwdriver, but I doubt it.

[2] doubt + Nominal Clause

(2a) I doubt if he ever travelled on a bus.

(2b) I doubt that she wrote the letter.

(2c) I doubt whether he is sane.

(2d) I doubt if he is honest.

(2e) I doubt whether it would work.

(2f) I doubt if Alan will meet her.

[3] Other Usage (with the adjective form)

(3a) He is doubtful about the future of the school

(3b) It is doubtful whether this will work

영작문제 :

a. 이자율(*interest rates*)이 곧 내려갈 것이라고 생각지 않는다. (내려갈 것을 의심한다.)

b. 나는 너를 의심한 적이 없다.

c. 많은 사람들이 그가 성공할 것(*his success*)을 의심했다.

d. 나는 신의 존재(*existence of God*)를 의심한 적이 없다.

e. 나는 그녀가 그 편지를 썼다는 것을 의심한다.

f. 그는 시험에서 부정행위를 했다고 의심받았다.

73. become

[1] become + Noun/Adjective

(1a) I became an engineer.

(1b) The ugly duckling became a beautiful swan.

(1c) Carol became a colorist for a children's animation company.

[2] become + Adjective

(2a) He became confused.

(2b) Things will become clearer in the morning.

(2c) He became annoyed when he heard the bad news.

[3] become + Preposition…

(3a) Children grew up to respect and become like their parents.

(3b) It didn't matter to her what became of us.

(3c) Where will he go to school now he's been thrown out of Eton? What will become of him?

[4] Other Usage

(4a) The new suit becomes(suits) you.

(4b) Shierlee's girl friends came to compliment her dress, a long, full-skirted silk which became her, both in color and in style.

영작문제 :

a. 그는 음악가가 되었다.

b. 그 피곤한 아이는 신경질적(*cranky*)이 되었다.

c. 내 우산은 어떻게 되었지?

74. come

[1] come + Ø/Adverb/Preposition…

(1a) My family must come first.

(1b) Come to me!

(1c) The children came reluctantly when I insisted.

(1d) Robin Dilk says the criticism comes at a time of mounting pressure on the government.

(1e) In 1962 there came the launching of the first Orbital Solar Observatory.

(1f) Tammy Johnson, a former drug addict, has come a long way.

(1g) A: How are things coming today?
B: They're coming fine.

(1h) Come to your senses!

(1i) Christmas comes but once a year.

(1j) Have you come across a book called 'The Fair Child?'

(1k) Would the wolves come after us?

(1l) The news came as a shock to me.

(1m) Such omissions hardly come as a surprise.

(1n) He came at me, hit me with the poker.

(1o) A good idea just came to me.

(1p) His attacker came for him with a broken glass and stabbed him in the face.

(1q) In this program, we talk to five people who come from all over the world.

(1r) Pendulums come in many different sizes and shapes.

(1s) Nothing came of these discussions.

(1t) Then the wheels started to come off the cart.

(1u) The economic reform proposals have already come under attack from the Russian leader, Boris Yeltsin.

(1v) That's certainly the case when it comes to issues like maps.

[2] come + Adjective

(2a) My dream came true.

(2b) I don't suppose your services come cheap.

(2c) The knot came loose.

[3] come + to-infinitive

(3a) She came to believe it.

(3b) Although it was a secret wedding, the press did eventually come to hear about it.

(3c) How did you come to meet him?

[4] Other Usage

(4a) Come see us. (Come and see us.)

(4b) I want you to come visit me. (come and visit me.)

영작문제 :

a. 그의 수입은 $500,000 이상에 이르렀다.

b. 그들은 의견일치(*agreement*)에 이르렀다.

c. 그는 자신이 실수했음을 깨닫게 되었다.

75. grow

[1] grow + Ø

(1a) Its economy was growing at a rapid rate.

(1b) The suspense grew.

(1c) He stopped growing at the age of 10.

[2] grow + Noun

(2a) I would love to create a garden and grow beautiful things.

(2b) I always grow a few red onions.

(2c) Lettuce was grown by the Ancient Romans.

[3] grow + Adjective

(3a) She grew quiet again.

(3b) He grew suspicious.

(3c) We are growing old.

(3d) The grass grows thin as you climb, revealing the bones of limestone.

(3e) I grew a little afraid of the guy next door.

[4] grow + to−infinitive

(4a) He grew to love his work.

(4b) Their friendship grew to be one of the happiest.

(4c) He grew to like her.

[5] grow + Preposition…

(5a) By then the group had grown to about ten members.

(5b) A lamb grows into a sheep.

(5c) The black unemployment grew from 11.8 per cent in 1970 to 21.1 per cent in 1981.

(5d) The boys grew into a men.

(5e) The idea for this book grew out of conversations with Philippa Brewster.

[6] Other Usage

(6) There is a whole generation in East Germany that grew up in a different political system.

영작문제 :

a. 결국(*after all*) 그는 나를 신뢰하게 되었다.

b. 그는 훌륭한 젊은이로 컸다.

76. put

[1] put + Noun + Adverb/Preposition···(Adverbial Phrase)

(1a) I put the book there.

(1b) He put the photograph on the desk.

(1c) He put the children to bed.

(1d) She put him in the hospital.

(1e) I would put you in the same category.

(1f) They are not prepared to put money into businesses in this country.

(1g) The governor has put a tax on cigarettes.

(1h) The lyrics had been put to music.

(1i) He put me through a lot of trouble.

(1j) The witness put the finger on the killer.

(1k) Let me put it simply. (express)

(1l) Let me put it this way.

(1m) I put my objections bluntly.

[2] Other Usage(Phrasal verbs)

(2a) Why not put aside your grudge?

(2b) Put all negative thoughts away.

(2c) I put in eight hours at the office.

(2d) I had to put off paying the bills.

(2e) They put out a fire.

(2f) She seems to have put on weight.

(2g) We've really had to put out to get this project finished.

(2h) We had to put up with the inconvenience.

(2i) He put me down for failing the course.

영작문제 :

a. 그는 책을 탁자 위에 놓았다.

b. 그는 손을 그의 호주머니에 넣었다.

77. bring

[1] bring + Noun

(1a) Remember to bring an apron or an old shirt to protect your clothes.

(1b) We don't know what the future will bring.

(1c) For Sandra, the new year brought disaster.

(1d) I am afraid I just cannot bring myself to talk about it at the moment.

[2] bring + Noun + Adverb/Preposition…(Adverbial Phrase)

(2a) My father brought home a book for me.

(2b) Her mother brought her hands up to her face.

(2c) I told you about what brought me here.

(2d) The shock of her husband's arrival brought her to her feet.

(2e) He is the one who brought the story to the world.

(2f) The incident brings the total of people killed to fifteen.

(2g) He went and poured a brandy for Elena and brought it to her.

(2h) He brought the car to a stop in front of the square.

(2i) I hope that the election will bring peace to Cambodians.

(2j) And that brings us to the end of this special report from Germany.

(2k) Dad brought a notebook along to the beach, in case he was seized by sudden inspiration.

[3] bring + Noun + Noun

(3a) The stewardess kindly brought me a blanket.

(3b) Her three children brought her joy.

(3c) We'll be bringing you all the details of the day's events.

[4] Other Usage(Phrasal verbs)

(4a) Someone went upstairs and brought down a huge kettle.

(4b) They brought along Laura Jane in a pram.

(4c) Other phrasal verbs : bring about, bring along, bring around, bring back, bring down, bring forward, bring in, bring off, bring on, bring out, bring round/around, bring to bring up, etc.

영작문제 :

a. 홍수(*floods*)가 그 계곡(*the valley*)을 파괴(*destruction*)시켰다. (홍수가 그 계곡에 파괴를 가져왔다.)

b. 이 음악은 추억(*memories*)을 일으키게 한다(*bring back*).

c. 그 연설은 여론(*public opinion*)에 있어서 변화(*a change*)를 가져왔다.

78. remain

[1] remain + Ø

(1a) Virtually nothing remained.

(1b) Very little of the house remained after the fire.

(1c) Only a few trees remained after the storm.

(1d) Despite the passing of so many years, the fond memories remain.

[2] There + remain + Noun

(2a) There remained only ten minutes. (⇐ There were only ten minutes remaining.)

(2b) There remained one significant problem.

(2c) There remains a large gulf between the limited agreement reached yesterday and putting it into practice.

[3] remain + Adjective/to-infinitive/Preposition…(Adjectival Phrase)

(3a) Much remains to be done.

(3b) Train fares are likely to remain unchanged.

(3c) It remains true that sport is about competing well, not winning.

(3d) It remains to be seen if they can do so without tearing each other apart.

(3e) Whether it's true or not remains to be found out.

(3f) Interest rates will have to remain at 14 per cent.

(3g) These matters remain in doubt.

(3h) A cure remains to be found.

[4] remain + Noun

(4a) It remains our aim to maintain its true value over the years.

(4b) Self catering remains an option at Youth Hostels for no extra charge.

(4c) In spite of their quarrel, they remain the best of friends.

(4d) He's been accused by the opposition of misleading the government over the crisis, and a general election remains a strong possibility.

[5] remain + Preposition(as)…

(5a) She will remain as prime minister.

(5b) He will remain as manager of the club until the end of his contract.

영작문제 :

a. 그는 집에 머물러 있었다.

b. Jane은 계속 유쾌한(*cheerful*) 모습을 보였다.

c. 그 문제는 아직 해결되지 않았다.

d. 그는 계속 침묵을(*silent*) 지켰다.

79. feel

[1] feel + Noun

(1a) I felt a sharp pain in my back.

(1b) The doctor felt my pulse.

(1c) He reached out and felt the wall.

(1d) Everyone felt the heat.

(1e) They felt the anger of the crowd.

[2] feel + Adjective

(2a) I feel a bit weak, that's all.

(2b) Mike felt able to take a risk.

(2c) I felt rejected and confused.

(2d) The water feels warm with the sun's rays pouring on it.

(2e) It was an accident; I feel awful about it.

(2f) The sheets felt smooth.

(2g) I felt uncomfortable.

[3] feel + Nominal Clause

(3a) I don't feel I've missed anything.

(3b) I feel he's guilty.

(3c) I remember feeling how helpless and vulnerable he looked.

(3d) It feels as if spring is in the air.

(3e) We all felt (that) we were unlucky to lose.

[4] feel + Preposition···

(4a) It's sad, I do feel for her.

(4b) I feel for you in your sorrow.

(4c) How are you feeling about the report you've got today?

(4d) I feel like a mouse being chased by a cat.

(4e) Whenever I felt like talking, they were ready to listen.

(4f) I feel like a cup of coffee.

(4g) I just don't feel like myself today.

(4h) Did having a gun make you feel like a man?

(4i) I don't feel up to going out tonight.

(4j) Whenever I felt like talking, they were ready to listen.

(4k) The interview only took ten minutes, but it felt like hours.

(4l) He felt in his pockets for some money.

[5] feel + Noun + to-infinitive/-ing/-ed/Noun complement

(5a) She felt his answer to be evasive.

(5b) I felt myself blushing.

(5c) I felt it necessary to ask for advice.

(5d) It just felt right for me to have an opportunity to go abroad and help other people.

(5e) She felt the boat moving.

(5f) As our eyes met for the first time I could feel my heart pounding.

(5g) Lucas could feel her staring at him.

(5h) He could feel the sweat pouring down his face.

(5i) She felt it her duty to tell the police.

[6] Other Usage

(6a) You really feel like you are in the Caribbean.

(6b) She felt the boat move.

(6c) This is something I feel strongly about.

영작문제 :

a. 그는 상자의 무게를 손으로 느껴 보았다.

b. 나는 피곤을(*tired*) 느꼈다.

c. 그 담요는 부드러웠다.

d. 나는 그가(*him*) 올 것처럼 느꼈다.

e. 나는 심장이 뛰는 것을 느꼈다.

f. 나는 집이 흔들리는 것을 느꼈다.

g. 집에 돌아와서(*It… to be home*) 기분 좋다.

h. 나는 우리가 사과해야 할(*have to apologize*) 것 같이 느꼈다.

80. smell

[1] smell + Ø

(1a) This closet smells.

(1b) His feet smell.

(1c) His clothes were always dirty and his body smelled.

[2] smell + Noun

(2a) She smelled the rose.

(2b) She smelled the meat to see if it was fresh.

(2c) She was smelling the flowers, early roses.

(2d) The detective smelled foul play.

[3] smell + Adjective

(3a) He didn't smell bad; he smelled clean and powdery.

(3b) That coffee smells good.

(3c) It smelled terrible.

(3d) It smelled good outside, clean and fresh and healthy.

[4] smell + Preposition…

(4a) The house smelled of flowers.

(4b) Doesn't it smell like a bakery in here, Howard?

(4c) The arrangement smelt like trap.

(4d) Both of those men had really smelled like cops to him.

(4e) The cage smelled of excrement and rancid sweat.

(4f) The dog was smelling around the bed.

[5] smell + Noun + −ing/−ed

(5a) Everyone likes to see and smell food being prepared.

(5b) I smell something burning.

(5c) I could smell the dinner cooking in the kitchen.

[6] Other Usage

(6a) He smelled as if he slept in the sewer.

(6b) Their breath smells like they have been eating catfish.

영작문제 :

a. 그 빵은 좋은 냄새가 난다.

b. 이 플라스틱은 가죽 같은(*like leather*) 냄새가 난다.

c. 나는 무언가가 썩고 있는 것을 느꼈다.

81. mention

[1] mention + Noun (+ Preposition…)

(1a) He did mention a price.

(1b) She asked me to mention her to Lloyd Plover.

(1c) Her death was not even mentioned.

(1d) In his speech, Sir Leon didn't mention Nicolas Ridley by name.

(1e) Nobody mentioned anything to me about it.

(1f) I mentioned your idea during the conversation.

(1g) Sorry, I won't mention it again.

[2] mention + Nominal Clause

(2a) He never once mentioned he had an injury problem.

(2b) Did he mention who their leader was?

(2c) I don't think I've mentioned to you that I've always fancied living in Bournemouth.

(2d) You mentioned in your letter that you might be moving abroad.

(2e) He failed to mention that he was the one who started the fight.

(2f) She mentioned that she was going to be five minutes late.

[3] Other Usage

(3a) Ella didn't mention knowing you.

(3b) One in five people mentioned using lead-free petrol as a possible cure.

(3c) Several people mentioned about asthma.

(3d) "Thank you very much." "Don't mention it."

영작문제 :

a. 그녀가 이것을 당신에게 언급했나요?

b. 그녀가 어디로 갈는지(*be going*) 말했나요?

c. 그는 다음 주 한국에 갈 것이라고 말했다.

82. mind

[1] mind + Ø

(1a) There are other things I'd rather talk about. Would you mind?

(1b) If nobody minds, I shall now leave you all to recover.

(1c) That's all right. I wouldn't mind.

(1d) You'll slip on the ice if you don't mind.

(1e) It was raining, but we didn't mind.

(1f) A: Would you rather go out or stay in?

B: I don't mind.

(1g) Never mind.

[2] mind + Noun

(2a) I did not mind the hard work; I was used to it and I liked it.

(2b) I don't mind the hunt, I mind the killing.

(2c) Eileen said she didn't mind cold coffee.

(2d) I don't mind the cold—it's the rain I don't like.

(2e) I hope you don't mind the noise.

(2f) Don't mind me. You two go head.

(2g) Never mind why, just stop.

(2h) Don't mind her—she didn't mean what she said.

(2i) Mind(Watch) that step! (British English)

(2j) Mind your language!

[3] mind + Preposition(about)···

(3a) Not that she was much good at cooking, but he didn't mind about that at all.

(3b) Never mind about that.

[4] mind + V–ing

(4a) I don't mind doing it.

(4b) Would you mind describing you background?

(4c) Do you mind being alone?

(4d) I wouldn't mind going to the cinema.

(4e) Would you mind explaining that again, please?

(4f) Do you mind driving? I'm feeling pretty tired.

(4g) I don't mind doing the chores when I don't feel rushed.

(4h) Would you mind turning your music down a little?

[5] mind + Nominal Clause

(5a) Do you mind that he's marrying Toni?
(5b) Never mind that people enjoy watching it.
(5c) I don't mind what job I do
(5d) He minded that he hadn't been asked.
(5e) Do you mind if I open the window?
(5f) Do you mind if I ask one more thing?

[6] mind + Genitive/Accusative pronoun (e.g. your/you) + V-ing

(6a) What sort of grade did you get, if you don't mind me asking?
(6b) She said she hoped you wouldn't mind her going through your things.
(6c) Do your parents mind your/you leaving home?
(6d) Are you married, if you don't mind my/me asking?

[7] Other Usage

(7) I don't mind it if she leaves us.

영작문제 :

a. 나는 힘든 일은 꺼려하지 않지만 보수가 적은 것은 싫다.
b. 나는 비속을 걷는 것을 개의치 않는다.
c. 담배 피워도 될까요?
d. 그녀는 그가 집에 늦게 오는 것을 개의치 않는다.

83. remind

[1] remind + Noun + Preposition(of, about)···

(1a) He reminded her of a dinner party the next night.

(1b) Flowers remind me of holidays.

(1c) You do not need to remind people of their mistakes.

(1d) He reminded himself of the strict timetable he was committed to.

(1e) His face reminded her of a frog.

(1f) She reminds me of her sister.

(1g) This reminds me of my schooldays.

(1h) The note was to remind him about something he had to explain to one or other of his students.

Grammar Tip 7 : 'Remind-동사'와 'Of'

'remind' 동사가 'of' 전치사와 함께 쓰일 때

: 'remind of something/someone'으로 쓰이고 'remind of doing'으로는 쓰이지 않는다.

---

[2] remind + Noun + Nominal Clause

(2a) Jim Brady came by yesterday to remind me we're going to an auction tomorrow.

(2b) I reminded him that we had a wedding to go to on Saturday.

(2c) His grin reminded me that I had been rude.

(2d) David reminded himself that he was on vacation.

(2e) Several times a day she would remind herself how lucky she was.

(2f) Correspondents are reminded that letters may be edited and shortened at the Editor's discretion.

[3] remind + Noun + to-infinitive

(3a) Please remind me to call you.

(3b) She reminded me to wear the visitor's badge at all times.

(3c) Can you remind me to buy a bottle of Martini?

[4] Other Usage

(4a) Thank you for reminding me.

(4b) I have to remind him how to mix her feeds.

(4c) When writing or editing, constantly remind yourself of who your readers are.

영작문제 :

a. 너의 아들은 그의 나이 때의 너(*you at his age*)를 생각나게 한다.

b. 그는 우리가 예전에 이곳을 방문했었다고 내게 상기시켜 주었다.

c. Tom은 Mary에게 감기약을 살 것을 상기시켰다.

84. report

[1] report + Ø (+ Preposition(to, from, for, on, etc.)…)

(1a) Barry Langridge of the BBC's Eastern Service now reports.

(1b) None of them had reported for duty.

(1c) She reports directly to the board of directors.

(1d) He reported for the Daily Echo for 40 years.

(1e) This is Jim Dale reporting from Chicago.

(1f) When you arrive, report to the receptionist.

(1g) He has to report to the police every five days.

(1h) Who do you report to?

(1i) Andrew Dunn reports on using a naturally occurring enzyme to destroy the AIDS virus.

[2] report + Noun (+ Preposition(to, from, on, etc.)…)

(2a) The study reported a decline in heart disease.

(2b) The committee reported the bill.

(2c) The couple reported the theft to the police.

(2d) His wife reported him to the police.

(2e) A burglar was reported in the area.

[3] report + Nominal Clause

(3a) The audit reports that the company lost money.

(3b) They reported that fallen tree limbs were blocking the road.

(3c) It's reported from Washington that Bulgaria is to send a military contingent to join the international forces already in the Gulf.

(3d) One journalist reported how he had trekked for three days through the jungle to interview the Karen guerrillas.

(3e) The deal is reported to be worth ninety-seven million dollars. (⇐ It is reported that the deal is worth ninety-seven million dollars. ⇐ They report that the deal is worth ninety-seven million dollars.)

(3f) She is reported to be in Italy. (⇐ It is reported that she is in Italy. ⇐ They report that she is in Italy.)

[4] report + Noun + Preposition(for)…

(4a) She had to report him for several minor incidents of sexual harrassment.

(4b) I suggest we report him for being drunk.

(4c) He refused to report another teacher to the head for an alleged misdemeanor.

[5] Other Usage

(5a) Would you please report on what happened?

(5b) Thirteen people were reported killed

(5c) I reported sick and was admitted to the sick bay with a temperature.

(5d) Residents of the Chinese capital Peking have reported seeing unusual movements of soldiers and armored vehicles around the city in recent days.

(5e) His parents reported him missing Jan. 4, a day after a Texas Highway Patrol officer stopped him for speeding in Amarillo, according to the missing person's report.

Grammar Tip 8 : 'It is reported that'과 문장부사 'reportedly'

앞서 제시된 동사들 'say, think' 등과 마찬가지로 'report' 동사는 목적절이 수동태가 되어 'It is reported that…' 구문을 형성할 수 있다. 이때도 역시 종속절의 주어가 전체 문장의 주어가 되어 사용될 경우 (3e)와 (3f)의 예문에서처럼 'to-부정사'가 오게 된다.

한편 'It is reported that…' 구문은 아래의 (1)과 (2)의 예에서 보듯이 간단하게 'reportedly'라는 문장부사(sentential adverb)로 대치되기도 한다. 이 때 문장부사 'reportedly'의 위치는 동사 뒤 혹은 문장 앞에도 올 수 있다.

(1) The deal is reportedly worth ninety-seven million dollars. (3e)

(2) She is reportedly in Italy. (3f)

영작문제 :

a. 그들은 John을 위원회에 보고하였다.

b. 신문은 그가 교통사고로 사망했다고 전했다.

c. i) 그가 전사하였다고(*be killed in the war*) 보도했다. (they를 주어로)

ii) 그가 전사하였다고 보도되었다.

d. i) 강풍(*the hurricane*)이 많은 사람들을 죽게 했다고 보도했다. (they를 주어로)

ii) 강풍(*the hurricane*)이 많은 사람들을 죽게 했다고 보도되었다.

85. seem

[1] seem + Adjective/Preposition…(Adjectival Phrase)

(1a) This seems nice.

(1b) The child seems healthy, but the doctor is concerned.

(1c) They seem in a hurry.

(1d) What seems clear is that the army have made significant advances.

(1e) Delegates seem certain to support Neil Kinnock's approach to the crisis.

(1f) This might not seem exciting to people who haven't used Mosaic before.

(1g) That didn't seem tacky to me at all.

(1h) This idea seems ridiculous to most people.

[2] seem + Noun

(2a) It seems a shame to leave right now.

(2b) Margaret seemed a gentle, well-adjusted woman.

(2c) It seemed a long time before the food came.

(2d) This may seem a surprising mixture, but eating sweet things with cheese is a tradition throughout Europe.

(2e) It seems a pity that so much flair and justment has been lavished on so narrowly alarming a set of preoccupation.

[3] seem + to-infinitive

(3a) The house seems to be in good condition.

(3b) The car seems to be running well.

(3c) They seem to miss the point.

(3d) Evidence seems to suggest that young drivers are far more likely to have accidents.

(3e) What seems to be the trouble?

(3f) The experiments seem to prove that sugar is bad for you.

(3g) It seems likely to rain.

[4] It + seems + Clause

(4a) It seemed to me that she was right.

(4b) It seems he went too far.

(4c) It seemed as though the war had ended.

(4d) For a moment, it seemed to her that he'd passed out.

(4e) It seemed to Anita as though two more strands, grey in hue, were not woven into the family tapestry.

(4f) It began to seem as if there was nothing we as individuals could do to help.

(4g) It seemed to me as though he had something unpleasant to tell me.

(4h) It always seemed as though they would get married.

[5] There + seem (+ to-infinitive) + Noun

(5a) There seems no need to go now.

(5b) There seemed to be no real coffee, but she found a bottle of instant in the pantry.

(5c) There seems no chance of him winning a majority.

[6] seem + Preposition(like) +-ing/Noun/Nominal Clause

(6a) He now seems like taking sides.

(6b) He seems like an honest man.

(6c) It doesn't seem like we're going to be very happy. (informal)

(6d) It seems like that the army will move in sometime today.

[7] Other Usage

(7) One of the Conservative party candidates, Alvaro Gomez, seems as though he would be quite happy not to win.

Grammar Tip 9 : 'It seems-구문'과 'There seem-구문'

A. 'It sems-구문'의 종속절의 주어가 주절의 주어로 쓰일 때 다음과 같이 'to-부정사'를 활용한 구문을 형성한다.

(1) It seems that they know what they're doing. [4]

(2) They seem to know what they're doing [3]

B. 'There is' 구문과 'seem to' 구문이 결합하여 본문 [5]의 'There seem (to be)' 구문이 사용된다.

(3a) It seems that there is no need to go now.

(3b) There seems (to be) no need to go now.

(4a) It seems that there is no chance of him winning a majority.

(4b) There seems (to be) no chance of him winning a majority.

영작문제 :

a. 그녀는 좋은 상사(*good boss*)처럼 보인다.

b. 그는 내게 항상 늙어 보인다.

c. 비가 올 것 같다(*It⋯ likely⋯*).

d. 집에 책을 놓고 온 것(*leave my book at home*) 같아.

e. 그에겐 어떤 타당한 대안(*reasonable alternative*)도 없는 것이 명확해 보인다.

f. 그는 모든 자신감을 잃어버린 것처럼 보인다.

g. 그녀가 영원히 가버린 것처럼 느껴진다.

h. 그에 대한 지지(*support*)가 많은 것처럼 보인다.

86. apply

[1] apply + Ø

(1a) All usual competition rules apply.

(1b) This information may not apply in Scotland, which has a different legal system.

[2] apply + Noun

(2a) Apply the cream evenly.

(2b) Charles Schumer said the US should apply pressure on its allies.

[3] apply + Preposition(to, for)...

(3a) I applied for a job there once.

(3b) The rule applies to everyone.

(3c) You have to apply in writing to Norfolk County Council for a permit.

영작문제 :

a. 그 새로운 기술(new technology)은 거의 모든 산업과정(industrial process)에 적용된다.

b. Tom은 그의 화학 지식을 그 문제에 적용했다.

c. 그는 미국대사관(the American embassy)에 비자를 신청했다.

87. spend

[1] spend + Noun

(1a) They spent their vacation in Paris.

(1b) Her husband had spent all her money.

(1c) I can never spend much money, so I buy from ethnic and second-hand shops.

[2] spend + Noun + Preposition(on, in)…

(2a) We always spend a lot of money on parties.

(2b) They spent all their resources on futile projects.

(2c) Some people spend more energy in attacking each other.

(2d) The buildings need a lot of money spent on them.

(2e) He spent considerable energy on convincing the former US administration that the educational process will have to be started all over again.

[3] spend + Noun + V−ing

(3a) I spent all day typing information into a computer.

(3b) They spent the night chatting intimately.

(3c) He spent an hour exercising.

(3d) She will spend her money installing a swimming pool at her second home in France.

(3e) Why had we spent so much energy competing with each other?

영작문제 :

a. 그는 많은 돈을 책에 쓴다.

b. 그는 한 달을 그 제안을 쓰면서(*write the proposal*) 보냈다.

88. try

[1] try + Ø

(1a) I know it's not easy, but keep trying!

(1b) You must try harder.

[2] try + Noun (+ Preposition(for, on)···)

(2a) Try ground chicken breast instead of beef in your burgers.

(2b) She tried her best to look cheerful.

(2c) You've only tried three questions.

(2d) He tries my patience.

(2e) He decided to try and solve his problems by himself.

(2f) I've tried the local library for information but to no avail.

(2g) I tried the idea on a couple of people, who greeted it with great enthusiasm.

(2h) Last year more than two thousand people were tried for trafficking in drugs.

(2i) He was tried, prosecuted and sent to prison for seven years for theft and deception.

[3] try + to-infinitive

(3a) My sister tried to cheer me up.

(3b) Some of the crowd tried to break through the police lines.

(3c) He tried to change the subject.

(3d) As far as she could tell, no one tried to find her.

(3e) They tried to persuade the police to impose a night curfew.

(3f) Please try to understand me.

(3g) Try to finish quickly

[4] try + V-ing

(4a) Don't try teaching us our business.

(4b) He tried changing the subject.

(4c) Try running a mile a day.

[5] try + Preposition(for, on)…

(5a) I want to try for the Presidency of the United States.

(5b) May I try this on?

[6] Other Usage (as a Noun)

(6a) The US negotiators decided to make another try at reaching a settlement.

(6b) I doubt they'll be able to help but it's worth a try.

(6c) I don't think I'll be any good at tennis, but I'll give it a try.

(6d) Why don't you have a try at convincing him?

영작문제 :

a. 이 커피 마셔 보시겠어요?

b. 그는 그녀를 진정시키고자(*calm her down*) 노력했다(시도했다).

c. 너 뭐하려는 중이니?

d. Charles는 절도(*theft*)혐의로 재판을 받았다.

89. understand

[1] understand + Ø

(1a) I don't want you doing that again. Do you understand?

(1b) They just don't understand.

(1c) I'm not sure that I understand. Go over it again.

(1d) If you want to leave early, I'm sure he'll understand.

[2] understand + Noun

(2a) Can you understand French?
(2b) She didn't understand the form she was signing.
(2c) Nobody understands me.
(2d) He doesn't understand women at all.
(2e) It is crucial that you understand the potential risks before surgery.
(2f) She could barely understand a word of English and she was talking Greek to people in the room.

[3] understand + Nominal Clause

(3a) They understand what I have been through.
(3b) I quite understand that you need some time alone.
(3c) I understand you wish to see the manager.
(3d) Am I to understand that you refuse?
(3e) You have to understand that he wants to create an empire for himself.
(3f) They must understand that many people need a certain freedom within a relationship.
(3g) He still couldn't understand why she was there.
(3h) She did not understand what was happening to her.
(3i) It is understood that the fee will be $50.
(3j) It is understood that the band are working on their next album.

(3k) It is understood that the British government decided on a new approach to the problem of shortages of teachers.

[4] Other Usage

(4) I can understand people getting very angry about violence against the person.

영작문제 :

a. 나는 그를 도저히(*not at all*) 이해할 수 없다.

b. 나는 왜 네가 그렇게 화가 났는지 이해할 수 없다.

c. 그가 심장마비를 앓았다고(*have a heart attack*) 한다.

i) 'we understand'로

ii) 'it'을 주어로

iii) 'he'를 주어로

90. estimate

[1] estimate + Noun

(1a) While an author is yet living, we estimate his powers by his worst performance.

(1b) Can you estimate my chances?

(1c) Can you estimate the price of this house?

(1d) This is what we estimate for the monthly repayments.

(1e) Perhaps the most useful section is the list of garden calculations estimating the amount of gravel required for a given area, for example.

[2] estimate + Nominal Clause

(2a) He estimated that the journey would take two hours.
(2b) We estimated it would cost about $50,000.
(2c) It is hard to estimate how many children suffer from dyslexia.
(2d) The Turkish authorities have been estimating how much the crisis is costing them in lost revenue.
(2e) Officials estimate it will be two days before electricity is restored to the island.
(2f) It has been estimated that the congestion is costing London's industry about 10 thousand million pounds a year.
(2g) It's estimated that twenty-five badgers are killed every day through the activity known as Badger Baiting.

[3] estimate + Noun + to-infinitive

(3a) I estimated the room to be 20 feet long.
(3b) I estimate this chicken to weigh three pounds.
(3c) The deal is estimated to be worth around $1.5 million.
(3d) Higher Education Price Index is estimated to drop but it still exceeds inflation.

[4] Other Usage

(4a) US State Department casualty figures estimate eighty nine people as being killed since Tuesday including seven civilians.

(4b) I estimated my chances of escape as very good.

(4c) His personal riches were estimated at over £8 million.

Grammar Tip 10 : 'Estimate-동사'의 특별한 용례

A. 'They(We) estimate that…' 문장은 종종 수동태로 쓰인다. 즉 일반주어를 갖고 있는 (1a)는 수동태인 (1b) 문장으로 쓰일 수 있다. 이 때 'It is estimated' 문장은 간단하게 문장부사로 대체될 수 있다. 즉 문장 대신 'estimatedly'라는 부사가 쓰여 문장을 간략하게 만들 수 있다. 이는 앞서 제시된 'reportedly'와 유사한 용례이며 본문에 제시된 동사 '*understand, suppose*'의 경우도 'It is understood/It can be understood,'와 'It is supposed'의 문장이 문장부사 'understandably'와 'supposedly'로 대체될 수 있다.

(1a) We estimate that the project will cost over five million dollars.

(1b) It is estimated that the project will cost over five million dollars.

(1c) The project will estimatedly cost over five million dollars.

B. (2a)와 같이 'There is' 구문과 'be estimated to' 구문이 결합될 수 있다. 이 때도 역시 문장부사가 쓰여 (2b)처럼 문장을 간략하게 만들 수 있다.

(2a) There are estimated to be some five hundred thousand West Germans who still own or have claims on property in East Germany.

(2b) There are estimatedly some five hundred thousand West Germans who still own or have claims on property in East Germany.

영작문제 :

a. 우리는 그 그림이 수천 불을 넘을 것으로 평가한다.

b. 그 그림의 가치가 수천 불을 넘는 것으로 평가된다.

c. 그 프로젝트가 4년 동안 지속될 것으로 평가된다.

i) 'it'을 주어로

ii) 'the project'를 주어로

C. 영어동사와 시제

대부분의 언어에서는 과거, 현재, 미래 등의 기본 시제를 사용하여 의미를 전달하고자 한다. 즉 과거의 특정 기간에 일어난 일을 의미할 때는 과거(Past) 시제가, 현재 일어나고 있거나 의례적인 일이거나 사실을 표현할 때는 현재(Present) 시제가 그리고 앞으로 일어날 일에 대해서는 미래(Future) 시제가 사용된다. 더불어 이 기본적인 세 가지 시제와 진행(Progressive)과 완료(Perfect)의 상(相, Aspect)이 함께 쓰인다. 즉 진행되고 있는 일을 서술할 때는 진행형이 쓰이며 이전의 시점에서 시작된 일이 특정 시점까지 지속되어 왔거나 그 시점을 기준으로 완료된 것을 의미하기 위해서는 완료형이 쓰인다. 이러한 진행형과 완료형은 과거, 현재, 그리고 미래의 기본 세 시제와 함께 복합적으로 쓰여 전체적인 영어 시제의 종류가 늘어나게 된다. 즉 영어에서는 과거, 현재, 미래의 세 기본 시제와 진행형, 완료형이 함께 조합되어 다양한 시제를 표현할 수 있다.

아래의 문장 (1a)는 현재의 상황에 대해 쓴 글이며 (1b)는 현재의 사실을 서술하고 있다. (2a)와 (2b)의 문장들은 '그가 세 달 전부터 McDonald's에서 계속 일해 왔고 현재에도 일하고 있다'는 정보를 제공한다. (3)는 단지 현재 그가 McDonald's에서 일하고 있는 중임을 표현하며 (4)는 현재완료와 진행형이 결합되어 '세 달 전부터 지금까지 쭉 McDonald's에서 일하고 있는 중'이라는 사실을 의미한다.

(1a) 현재시제 : He works at McDonald's.
(1b) 현재시제 : London is the capital of Britain.
(2a) 현재 + 완료 : He has worked there for three months now.
(2b) 현재 + 완료 : He has worked there since three months ago.
(3) 현재 + 진행 : He is working at McDonald's.
(4) 현재 + 완료 + 진행 : He has been working there for three months now.

이는 과거시제의 경우에도 마찬가지이다. 아래의 (5a)는 단순히 과거의 어느 시점에 McDonald's에서 일했다는 의미로 현재 상황에 대한 정보는 전혀 없으며 (5c)는 과거 특정기간 동안 일하고 있었다는 의미를 갖는다. 그러나 (5b) 문장은 (과거시제 이전의) 7월부터 과거의 특정 시점까지 그곳에서 근무했었다는 정보를 제공하며 (5d) 문장은 (5b)에 진행형이 첨가되어 과거 이전부터 과거시점까지 쭉 일하고 있어 왔었다는 의미를 뜻한다.

(5a) 과거시제 : He worked at McDonald's.
(5b) 과거 + 완료 : He had worked there since July.
(5c) 과거 + 진행 : He was working at McDonald's.
(5d) 과거 + 완료 + 진행 : He had been working since July.

미래시제의 경우 앞으로 일어날 일을 예상하는 데 쓰이며 (9)이나 (10)의 문장처럼 진행형이 가까운 미래의 확실한 일을 의미하기도 한다. 또한 (11)~(13)에서처럼 미래에 일어날 일이지만 늘 일어나는 일이나 습관 스케줄의 경우 현재시제를 쓴다. 한편 미래완료는 서술하는 일이나 행동이 언제

시작되었건 상관없이 미래의 어느 시점에 그 일이나 행동이 완료되거나 그 때까지 지속되는 것을 의미한다. 따라서 (14)의 문장은 '이전부터 쭉 이곳에서 살아 왔으며 미래의 특정 시점인 다음 크리스마스 시점에는 여기서 10년을 살게 된다'라는 의미를 갖는다.

(6) I'll see you tomorrow.

(7) It will be a nice day tomorrow.

(8) I'm going to drive to work today.

(9) He's meeting Peter in town this afternoon.

(10) I'm playing football tomorrow.

(11) We have a lesson next Monday.

(12) The train arrives at 6.30 in the morning.

(13) The holidays start next week.

(14) By next Christmas we will have been here for 10 years.

전반적으로 일반시제와 완료시제의 가장 큰 차이점은 일반시제는 현재나 과거 혹은 미래 시점의 행동이나 사건에 대해 말할 뿐 과거이전과 과거, 과거와 현재 그리고 미래 사이에 대한 어떤 정보도 제공하지 않는다. 가령 과거시제와 현재완료 시제를 비교하면 앞의 (5a) 문장의 과거시제는 과거시점에 대해서만 정보를 제공하는 반면 (2a)와 (2b)문장에서 사용된 현재완료 시제는 과거의 특정 시점(3달 전)부터 현재까지 어떤 일이 있었는지를 말하고 있다. 즉 현재완료 시제는 과거에 일어난 일이 현재 어떠한 상황인지 알려줌으로써 현재와 과거를 잇는 역할을 한다.

한편 영어의 시제는 복합절(Complex sentence)에서 현재시제가 미래시제 대신에 사용되기도 한다. 즉 (15)~(18)에 주어진 문장들처럼 주절(Main sentence)과 종속절이 같은 미래시제를 나타낼 때 주절에는 미래시제가 표시되지만 종속절에는 미래조동사를 생략하여 현재시제가 미래시제를 표현한다. 이는 주절의 미래시제를 통하여 종속절도 미래시제를 나타내고 있음을 예측할 수 있기 때문이다. 또한 (19)의 주동사 'hope'나 명령문처럼 앞으로 일어날 일에 대해 이야기하는 동사의 경우 현재시제가 미래시제를 대신해서 사용되기도 한다.

(15) I'll phone you when I get home. (I ~~will~~ get home)

(16) If Barcelona wins tomorrow, they will be champions. (Barcelona ~~will~~ win tomorrow)

(17) I'll come home as soon as I have finished work. (I ~~will~~ have finished work)

(18) You will be tired out after you have been working all night. (you ~~will~~ have been working)

(19) I hope he will recover/recovers soon.

앞서 wish-동사의 용례와 관련하여 설명하였듯이 가정법은 실제와 반대의 일이나 행동을 표현하기 위해 시제를 이용하는 독특한 표현법이다. 즉 가정법과거는 현재 사실의 반대를 의미하여 현재 일에 대해 아쉬워하거나 후회하는 마음을 표현할 때 사용되며 과거시제를 활용해서 일반 서술문과 구분되도록 하며 가정법 과거완료는 과거 사실의 반대 즉 이루어 지지 않았던 일에 대해 아쉽거나 후회했던 마음을 표현할 때 과거완료시제를 활용해서 일반 서술문과 구분되도록 한다.

(20) If David was here, he would know what to do. (가정법 과거 : 현재 사실의 반대)

(21) If she could see him now, she'd be so proud. (가정법 과거 : 현재 사실의 반대)

(22) I would have helped him if he had asked. (가정법 과거완료 : 과거 사실의 반대)

원칙적으로 본동사가 아닌 동사에는 시제를 구분해서 표시하지 않는다. 가령 분사구문의 동사, 조동사 뒤의 원형동사, 부정사, 그리고 동명사는 일반 동사들처럼 과거, 현재, 미래의 시제구분이 없다. 그러나 본동사와 시제의 일치를 보이지 않을 경우 극히 제한적으로 시제를 표시할 수 있으며 바로 다음과 같은 경우에 시제구분을 한다. 즉 아래의 예에서 보듯이 문장의 본동사보다 이전에 일어난 행동이나 사건을 의미하도록 시제를 구분해서 표현할 수 있다. 즉 (23)과 (24)의 문장에서 'to have lost'와 'having put'은 각각 본동사 'seem'과 'set off'보다 이전에 일어난 일을 표현하고 있다.

(23) He seems to have lost interest in you.

(24) Having put on his hiking boots, he set off down the trail.

다른 제한된 시제의 사용의 예로 조동사의 과거형을 고려할 수 있다. 'could, should, would, might' 등의 조동사는 과거시제로 쓰여 간접적이거나 좀 더 예의바른(polite) 표현에 사용되기도 한다. 그 예들은 다음과 같다.

(25) Would you kindly help me with this baggage?

(26) Could you open the door for me, please?

(27) Could I go now if you would not mind?

(28) I might have to go now.

(29) Might I speak to you for a moment?

시제와 관련된 연습문제

※ 다음의 문장을 의미에 맞게 시제를 적용하여 영작하시오.

(1) 봄이 왔다. (현재 봄인 것을 의미)

(2) 다음 달 Jane이 여기 오면 그녀를 만날 것이다.

(3) James는 2011년 5개월 동안 New York에서 살았다.

(4) James는 2011년부터 (지금까지) New York에서 산다.

(5) James는 2011년부터 (지금까지) New York에서 살고 있는 중이다.

(6) 몇 시간 동안이나 비가 오고 있다.

(7) 모두들 우리를 기다리고 있을 거야.

(8) 내가 파티에 도착했을 때는 Shelley는 이미 떠나고 없었다.

(9) 나는 유럽에 가 본 적이 없다.

(10) 다음 싱가포르 행 비행기는 오후 5시에 출발할 예정이다.

(11) 그녀가 지금 그를 볼 수 있다면 무척 자랑스러워 할 텐데…

(12) 나는 오늘 오후 buyer들과 만날 것이다/만날 계획이다/만나기로 되어 있다.

(13) 브라질이 월드컵 우승을 할 것 같다.

(14) 2012년 겨울은 매우 추웠다.

(15) 그녀는 십대였을 때부터 쭉 발레를 해 왔다.

(16) 그녀가 그를 볼 수 있었다면 무척 자랑스러워했을 텐데…

II

명사의 수식어

II 명사의 수식어

A. 명사와 한정사

지금까지 문장의 서술부를 담당하는 동사와 그와 관련된 문장구조를 살펴보고 연습하였다. 본 장에서는 문장의 주어나 동사의 목적어, 보어 등의 기능을 담당하는 명사(Noun)와 그 명사를 수식하는 다양한 수식어(Modifier)에 관해 살펴보고 그 용례를 익히고자 한다.

영어의 명사의 종류는 크게 셀 수 있는 가산명사(Countable Noun)와 수를 셀 수 없는 불가산명사(Uncountable Noun)로 구분될 수 있다. 가령 'assignment' 같은 가산명사는 문장 안에서 한정적인 의미로 쓰이지 않을 경우 단수인 경우 'an assignment'로, 그리고 복수인 경우에는 '하나의…'를 의미하는 부정관사 'a/an'과 의미상으로 충돌하므로 부정관사 없이 'Ø assignments'로 쓰인다. 한편 한정적 의미로 쓰일 때는 'the assignment, the assignments' 등의 정관사와 함께 쓰인다.

반면에 'homework' 같은 불가산명사는 셀 수 없는 명사이므로 단수나 복수의 개념과 어울리지 않아 복수형으로 쓰일 수 없는 관계로 부정관사 없이 'Ø homework'로 쓰이며 한정적 의미일 때 'the homework'로 쓰인다. 한편 영어 명사들 중에는 문맥에 따라 가산명사로도 쓰이고 불가산명사로도 쓰이는 명사들이 있으므로 항상 의미와 함께 문장을 통해 익혀야 한다. 다음은 일부 가산명사와 불가산명사의 용례를 보여주는 예들이다.

(1) Ø Milk is very good for you.

(2) Ø Health and Ø education are very important.

(3) A woman was lifted to Ø safety by a helicopter.

(4) Ø Girls normally do better in Ø school than Ø boys.

(5) The girls in TJ high school are excellent in many subjects.

(6) This news is very important.

명사를 수식하는 다양한 요소들 중에는 관사(Article)를 포함하는 한정사(Determiner)들과 형용사가 있다. 관사의 경우 막연하게 '하나의…'의 의미로 가산명사를 처음 소개할 경우 부정관사와 함께 쓰이며 불가산명사는 관사 없이 쓰인다.

반면에 앞서 언급한 명사를 다시 언급하거나 의미상 형용사구나 형용사절이 수식하며 한정할 때 정관사가 쓰인다. 혹은 처음 언급하는 명사일지라도 문맥이나 상황을 통해 어떤 것을 지칭하는지 알 수 있을 경우에도 정관사가 쓰인다. 다음의 문장들은 관사의 용례를 보여준다.

(7) Please remember to bring an umbrella. (우산 (아무거나) 꼭 가져가렴.)

(8) I love your pen. Please give me the pen. (아무 펜이 아닌 특정 펜(내가 정말 좋아하는 너의 펜)을 지칭함.)

(9) Yesterday I saw a beautiful girl. (한 소녀를 처음 봄.)

(10) Yesterday I saw the beautiful girl. (내가 전에 언급했던 그 아름다운 소녀)

(11) This morning I had an accident. (오늘 아침에 사고가 났다. 즉 새로운 사고인 만큼 부정관사를 씀.)

(12) Have you fully recovered from the accident? (특정 사고로부터 회복되었는지를 질문함.)

(13a) Pass me the salt please. (처음 언급하더라도 듣는 사람이 어떤 것을 가리키는지 이해한다고 가정하고 정관사를 씀.)

(13b) China's been gaining on Japan for years and as it has grown, the country has become aggressive in asserting its interests. (마찬가지로 여기서도 'country'는 처음 언급하는 단어이지만 앞에 나온 China를 지칭하는 것임을 미루어 짐작할 수 있기 때문에 정관사를 씀.)

(14) He is the player to watch in this game. (형용사구 'to watch'가 뒤에서 수식함으로써 '주시해야 할 특정한 선수'를 뜻함.)

(15) Do you have a dictionary that I can borrow? (뒤에 수식어가 있어도 아무 사전이나 '사전 하나'를 뜻하므로 부정관사를 씀.)

(16) Did you read the book that I bought you? (내가 사 준 그 책을 뜻함.)

한정사에는 관사들 이외에도 'his, her, its, their' 등의 소유대명사(Possessives), 'this, that, these, those' 등의 지시사(Demonstratives), 'which, what, whose' 등의 의문사(Interrogatives) 등이 있다. 명사를 수식하는 다른 한정사들로는 'all, every, few, little, any, most, some, one, two…' 등 수식하는 명사의 수나 양, 정도를 나타내는 다양한 한정사들이 있으며 이러한 한정사들은 (17)과 (18)번 예들에서 보듯이 형용사 앞에 위치한다. 또한 주의할 것은 이러한 한정사들 중에 중복해서 사용되지 않는 조합이 있는데 관사, 소유대명사, 지시사들은 중복해서 사용되지 않는다. 즉 (21)과 (22)의 예처럼 쓰이지 않는다. 그러나 다른 한정사들은 중복해서 사용되기도 한다. 한편 (26b)는 중복해서 사용될 수 있는 한정사들을 전치사 'of'로 갈라놓은 잘못된 표현이며 이렇게 전치사가 들어갈 경우는 (26c)와 같이 정관사, 지시대명사 혹은 소유대명사가 명사 앞에 수식할 경우에만 해당된다. 이 때 전치사 앞의 'most'는 대명사(Pronoun)로 사용된다.

(17) He read the exciting adventure movie.

(18) Look at those lovely flowers.

(19) Thank you very much for your letter.

(20) Whose coat is this?

(21) a ~~my~~ friend (a friend of mine)

(22) ~~the my~~ school (the school of mine)

(23) We meet every few days.

(24) I've read all six novels by Jane Austen.

(25) Have you got any more coffee?

(26a) Most people agree with me.

(26b) (X) Most of people agree with me.

(26c) Most of the people agree with me.

명사 및 수식어와 관련된 연습문제

※ 다음의 문장들 중 밑줄 친 명사나 명사구를 주어진 한글 번역에 맞게 적절한 수식어를 사용하여 고쳐 적으시오. (관사를 포함한 한정사를 정확하게 고쳐 적으시오.)

(1) Neighbor saw her talking with the George. (한 이웃이 그녀가 George와 말하고 있는 것을 보았다.)

(2) We were talking about movie all night. (우리는 밤새도록 영화에 대해서 이야기 하였다.)

(3) Cold weather caused plant die. (그 추운 날씨 때문에 화초가 죽었다.)

(4) He felt boy's weight with hand. (그는 그 소년의 무게를 손으로 느껴보았다.)

(5) That's a useful information. (그거 유용한 정보네.)

(6) They have beautiful house. (그들은 멋진 집을 갖고 있다.)

(7) We saw very exciting film last night. (우리는 어제 밤 아주 흥미로운 영화를 보았다.)

(8) He gave me some useful advices. (그는 내게 몇몇 유용한 충고를 했다.)

(9) Man climbing nearby saw accident. (근처에서 산에 오르고 있던 남자가 사고현장을 목격했다.)

(10) We bought some used furnitures. (우리는 중고가구 몇 개를 샀다.)

(11) Teacher encouraged her to write short story. (선생님은 그녀가 단편 소설을 쓰도록 격려했다.)

(12) He has reason to be mad. (그는 화낼만한 이유가 있다.)

(13) A hail is dangerous for driving. (우박은 운전에 위험하다.)

(14) He has a my car today. (그가 오늘 내 차를 운전하고 있다.)

(15) They had to spend night in hotel because a flight was cancelled. (그들은 그들이 타려던 비행편이 취소되어 호텔에서 하루 밤을 지내야 했다.)

B. 명사를 수식하는 형용사구

영어에서 명사를 앞에서 수식하는 요소들은 앞서 언급한 한정사들과 형용사들이다. 그러나 문장의 의미상 종종 구나 절이 명사를 수식해야 하는 경우가 발생하는데 이때 이러한 형용사구와 형용사절은 수식하는 명사의 뒤에 위치하게 된다. 형용사구에는 'to-부정사, 전치사구, 그리고 형용사절에서 유래된 -ing/-ed형' 등이 있다. 아래의 예들 중 (16)과 (17)은 명사 뒤에 'to-부정사'가, (18)과 (19)의 예들은 전치사구가 형용사구로 쓰여 수식받는 경우이다. (20)~(23)의 예들에서는 '-ing'와 '-ed'형의 형용사구가 쓰여 앞의 명사를 수식하고 있다.

(16) the desire to kill

(17) the time to heal

(18) a girl in a dark grey dress

(19) the house of ghosts

(20) a Web site containing a database

(21) the laws governing the physics of light

(22) a room filled with dozens of toys

(23) the land devastated by storms

영어 명사는 또한 문장이 수식하기도 한다. 수식받는 명사의 뒤에 와서 수식하는 형용사절 즉 관계절에 대해서는 III장에서 논의될 것이다.

형용사구와 관련된 연습문제

※ 주어진 의미에 맞게 영어로 표현하시오.

(1) 논의할 주제 (*discuss, topic*)

(2) 교복을 입은 한 여자 아이 (*uniform*)

(3) 500만 회원을 보유하고 있는 인터넷 카페

(4) 1980년대의 전설 (*legend*)

(5) 애국영화 (*patriotism*)

(6) 세계를 움직이는 힘

(7) 주목해야 할 논문 (*paper, notice*)

(8) 대중매체의 힘 (*mass media*)

(9) 손이 세 개 달린 괴물 (*monster*)

(10) 두 마을 사이의 길

III

복합절의 이해와 활용

III 복합절의 이해와 활용

언어를 사용할 때는 당연히 두 개 이상의 절을 사용하여 의사를 표현할 필요가 종종 생긴다. 즉 시간이나 조건, 이유, 양보 등의 부가적인 의미를 표현하기 위해 부사절을 사용하기도 하고 절이 주어, 보어 그리고 목적어의 명사절로 쓰이기도 한다. 또한 절이 명사를 수식하는 형용사절 혹은 관계절을 구성하기도 한다. 본 장에서는 이와 같은 두 개 이상의 문장이 구성하는 복합절을 이해하고 복합절을 활용하여 영어문장을 구사하는 연습을 하고자 한다.

A. 접속의 종류

두 개 이상의 문장을 사용하는 것을 접속(Conjunction)한다고 하며 절의 접속에는 등위접속(Coordinating Conjunction)과 종속접속(Subordinate Conjunction)이 있다. 단순히 두 문장을 이어놓는 등위접속은 A라는 문장과 B라는 문장 사이에 접속사를 위치하여 두 문장을 연결하는 것이다. 따라서 등위절은 (1b)나 (2b)처럼 접속사가 앞에 나올 수 없다. 등위절을 이끄는 접속사들은 '*and, but, or, so, yet, nor, for*' 등이 있다. 한편 (3)과 (4)의 예처럼 등위절에서 두 문장에서 중복되는 부분은 생략될 수 있다.

(1a) They are living in England, or they are spending a vacation there.

(1b) (X) Or they are spending a vacation there, they are living in England.

(2a) Because he was unhappy, he asked to be transferred.

(2b) (X) For he was unhappy, he asked to be transferred.

(3) I may see you tomorrow or may phone late in the day.

(4) I want to play the guitar and to sing better.

(5) Suddenly it began to rain, so I went back home.

(6) They don't gamble, nor do they smoke.

(7) They gamble, yet they don't smoke.

(8) They gamble, but they don't smoke.

이 외에도 (9)에서 (13)까지의 예처럼 보통 유사한 요소를 연결해 놓은 문장들을 상관접속(Correlative Conjunction)이라고 하며 상관접속을 구성하는 표현으로는 '*either~or~, neither~nor~, not~but~, not only(just)~but (also)~, as~as~, just as~so~, the more(less)~the more(less)~, no sooner~than~, so~as~, whether~or~, both~and~*' 등이 있다.

(9) Either do your work or prepare for a trip to the office.

(10) Not only is he handsome but he is also brilliant.

(11) Neither the basketball team nor the football team is doing well.

(12) Both the cross country team and the swimming team are doing well.

(13) Whether you stay or go is your decision.

반면에 종속접속(Subordinate Conjunction)은 복합절이 주절과 종속절로 구분되는 문장이다. (14)는 절이 told의 목적어로 쓰인 명사절이고 (15)는 이유를 나타내는 부사절을 갖는 복합절이며 (16)은 뒤의 관계절이 앞의 명사 'a woman'을 수식하는 형용사절에 해당된다.

(14) I told him that he was crazy. (명사절)

(15) As it's raining again, we'll have to stay at home. (부사절)

(16) I met a woman who likes to go to a rock concert. (형용사절)

B. 부사절

B-1. 부사절의 용례

부사절은 시간, 조건, 양보, 이유 등을 나타내는 종속절이다. 등위절과 달리 종속절인 부사절은 문장의 앞과 뒤에 위치할 수 있다. 아래의 문장들은 시간을 나타내는 부사절이 종속절로 쓰인 예들이다. 특히 문장 (1)에서처럼 종속절인 부사절이 주절 앞에 올 경우 의미상 종속절에 속하기 때문에 대명사가 주절의 명사보다 앞서 사용되기도 한다. 보통 대명사는 앞서 소개된 명사를 언급하기 위해 쓰이기 때문에 제시된 명사의 뒤에 쓰이나 이 경우 부사절이 종속절이므로 대명사가 주절의 해당 명사보다 먼저 사용되는 것이다.

(1) When he came in here as a freshman, Corey Fisher was the least prepared to be a leader.

(2) As the ranger was issuing us our permit, he warned us of the bears.

(3) I held the flashlight while my brothers were setting up the tent.

(4) It was dark when my two brothers and I arrived at the station.

(5) After we had put on our hiking boots, we set off down the trail.

(6) Before we set off down the trail, we put on our hiking boots.

(7) I stayed in my tent until it was light outside. (Then she left the tent.)

(8) Ever since he was a child, Jim has had the tendency to get angry easily.

(9) We'll go to lunch when you come to visit.

부사절을 이끄는 접속사에는 위의 예들처럼 하나의 접속사가 이끄는 것들뿐만 아니라 아래에서 보듯이 여러 단어가 복합적으로 사용되어 파생된 것들도 있다.

(10) During the time that we remained in the tent, I was very frightened.

(11) From the moment I first saw her, I have been in love with her.

(12) As soon as we arrived at a small clearing, we began to set up camp.

(13) I turn on the television set the moment that I get home.

(14) Whenever he comes, we go to have lunch at "Dick's".

(15) We take a hike every time he visits.

(16) The first time I went to New York, I was intimidated by the city.

(17) I saw Jack the last time I went to San Francisco.

(18) The second time I played tennis, I began to have fun.

다음은 조건, 이유 및 인과관계와 관련된 의미의 부사절을 이끄는 접속사들과 그 예들이다.

(19) In the case you need me, I'll be at Tom's.

(20) Whether they have money or not, they won't be able to come.

(21) I'll be studying upstairs in the event he calls.

(22) We'll give you your bicycle only if you do well on your exams.

(23) If we win, we'll go to Kelly's to celebrate!

(24) Once I arrive in Hong Kong, I am going to visit my friend's parents.

(25) Now (that) I am out of college, I must be on my own.

(26) Unless she hurries up, we won't arrive in time.

(27) As long as you have the time, why don't you come for dinner?

(28) Since he loves music so much, he decided to go to a conservatory.

(29) They received a high mark on their exam because they had studied hard.

(30) As the test is difficult, you had better get some sleep.

(31) We will be staying for an extra week due to the fact that we have not yet finished.

한편 접속사 '*even though, though, although, whereas, while*' 등은 주절과 상반되는 내용의 양보절(Concessive Clause)을 이끈다.

(32) Even though it was expensive, he bought the car.

(33) Though he loves doughnuts, he has given them up for his diet.

(34) Although the course was difficult, he passed with the highest marks.

(35) Whereas you have lots of time to do your homework, I have very little time indeed.

(36) Mary is rich, while I am poor.

B-2. 부사절의 부사구로의 전환

부사절은 때때로 접속사와 주어를 비롯한 주절과 중복되는 내용을 생략하여 간략한 부사구로 표현하기도 하는데 이를 분사구문(Participle Construction)이라고 한다. 아래 문장들 중 (b)의 예들은 분사구문으로 쓰인 문장들이며 일반적으로 종속절의 접속사, 중복되는 주어, 그리고 수동태의 'be-동사'가 생략되며 남은 동사는 능동의 경우 현재분사로, 수동의 경우 과거분사의 형태로 쓰여 구를 형성한다. 즉 이때 생략되는 부분은 거꾸로 다시 절의 형태로 만들 때 예측 가능한 잉여적인 부분에 해당되며 생략되었다가 회복되기 힘든 요소는 절대로 생략되지 않는다. 즉 (1a)의 복합절 중 종속절의 접속사와 주절과 공통되는 주어가 생략되고 능동형 동사 'love'에 현재분사형 '-ing' 접사를 붙여 (1b)와 같이 부사구가 만들어진다. 또한 생략되는 접속사의 경우도 특별한 의미를 갖는 접속사들이 아닌 이유, 때, 조건, 양보 등을 나타내는 일반적인 접속사들에 국한된다.

(1a) Since he loves music so much, he decided to go to a conservatory.
(1b) Loving music so much, he decided to go to a conservatory.
(2a) After we had put on our hiking boots, we set off down the trail.
(2b) Having put on our hiking boots, we set off down the trail.
(3a) When he wrote the cover letter, he sent it to the company.
(3b) Writing the cover letter, he sent it to the company.
(4a) Because she found herself lost, she asked a passerby for directions.
(4b) Finding herself lost, she asked a passerby for directions.
(5a) If it is held steady, the ship will be able to navigate through the storm.
(5b) Held steady, the ship will be able to navigate through the storm.

B-3. 부사절의 내용을 담는 문장부사

영어문장들을 읽다보면 '*-ly*'의 형태의 부사어를 자주 접하게 된다. 이들 중 상당수는 문장으로 해석될 수 있는 것들이다. 즉 '*It is* [Adjective/V-ed(수동태 과거분사)] *that*'과 같은 문장이 문장부사로 단순화되기도 한다. 가령 '*It is apparent that*' 같은 표현은 '*apparently*'로, '*It is alleged that*'은 '*allegedly*'와 같이 부사로 표현해서 부사절을 한 단어로 줄임으로써 복문을 단문으로 줄일 수 있다. 이처럼 문장에서 파생된 부사를 문장부사(Sentential Adverb)라고 한다. 아래의 예들은 다양한 문장부사를 보여준다. 따라서 영어문장에서 이러한 문장부사를 사용하여 보다 간략한 문장을 만들곤 한다.

(1a) <u>It is clear that</u> the Bradys is a happy family.

(1b) <u>Clearly</u> the Bradys is a happy family.

(2a) <u>It is apparent that</u> Jane and you are still friends.

(2b) Jane and you are <u>apparently</u> still friends.

(3a) <u>It is obvious that</u> it doesn't make sense to say Ms. John Jones.

(3b) <u>Obviously</u>, it doesn't make sense to say Ms. John Jones.

(4a) <u>It is surprising that</u> Asian, not Latin American, students make up the largest foreign contingent in the Lone Star State's colleges and universities.

(4b) <u>Surprisingly</u>, Asian, not Latin American, students make up the largest foreign contingent in the Lone Star State's colleges and universities.

(5a) <u>It is undeniable that</u> he was handsome, graceful and well-bred.

(5b) He was <u>undeniably</u> handsome, graceful and well-bred.

(6a) It is odd that softball was always regarded as a great game for girls and women.

(6b) Oddly, softball was always regarded as a great game for girls and women.

(7a) And it is more important that all the institutions in society at the time was pushing a certain model of the family.

(7b) And more importantly, all the institutions in society at the time was pushing a certain model of the family.

(8a) It is natural that restaurants prefer that you do choose an entrée.

(8b) Naturally, restaurants prefer that you do choose an entrée.

(9a) It is fortunate that we live in a very open society.

(9b) We live, fortunately, in a very open society.

(10a) It is unfortunate that many moms have to work.

(10b) Unfortunately, many moms have to work.

(11a) It is inevitable that the conversation at the end of any euchre round turns to a dizzying analysis of who played what, when and why.

(11b) The conversation at the end of any euchre round inevitably turns to a dizzying analysis of who played what, when and why.

(12a) It is indisputable that softball is the great national game and passion.

(12b) Softball is indisputably the great national game and passion.

(13a) It is reported that Google is preparing to announce the software at next month's Google I/O conference.

(13b) Google is reportedly preparing to announce the software at next month's Google I/O conference.

(14a) It is alleged that the suspect was involved in the robbery, but his alibi placed him in another state at the time.

(14b) The suspect was allegedly involved in the robbery, but his alibi placed him in another state at the time.

(15a) According to your testimony, it is supposed that you were at home watching TV when the murder occurred.

(15b) According to your testimony, you were supposedly at home watching TV when the murder occurred.

C. 명사절

C-1. 명사절의 용례

명사절은 문장 안에서 명사가 하는 기능인 주어, 보어, 그리고 목적어로 쓰인다. 명사절은 보통 접속사 '*that*'이 이끌거나 의문사가 이끈다. (1)~(8)의 문장들은 명사절이 동사의 목적어로 쓰인 경우이다. 특히 (7)과 (8)에서는 앞의 'be concerned about'과 '*be interested in*' 같은 구문의 목적어로 쓰였다. (9)에서 (11)은 명사절이 주어로 쓰인 예이며 특히 (10)과 (11)의 문장은 주어가 너무 긴 것을 피하려는 영어의 속성 상 가주어 'it'로 대체되어 쓰인 경우이다. (12)와 (13)은 명사절이 보어로 쓰인 예들이다.

(1) I think (that) he is a liar.

(2) He said that the strike wasn't over yet.

(3) He replied that they were on strike.

(4) He didn't say whether the president was going to cooperate.

(5) I don't know what he wants. (⇐ "What does he want?")

(6) The reporter asked Mr. Foster who was on strike.

(7) We are concerned about whether (or not) he is telling the truth.

(8) She is interested in how many people are striking.

(9) What they want is a state of their own.

(10) It is necessary that he should become aware of the situation.

(11) It is important that he should be on time to class.

(12) The truth is that even on a normal day, New Orleans is a sad city.

(13) This is what they want.

C-2. 의문절의 명사절

동사의 목적어로 의문절이 올 때는 그 의문절은 조동사 'do'가 빠지고 주어와 동사의 위치가 서술문의 어순처럼 쓰인다. 즉 아래의 예에서 [조동사 'do' + 주어] 어순의 의문문 (1a)는 (1b)의 문장에서 동사의 목적절이 될 때 'do'가 생략되고 어순은 [주어 + 동사]가 된다. 물론 (4)와 (5)의 예들에서 보듯이 의문사가 주어일 때는 의문절 자체에서 [주어 + 동사]의 어순을 갖게 되므로 변화가 없다.

(1a) What do you want?

(1b) I asked him what he wanted.

(2a) What are you talking about?

(2b) I don't know what you are talking about.

(3a) Did you hear the news?

(3b) She asked me if I heard the news.

(4a) Who's coming?

(4b) Do you know who's coming?

(5a) What happened?

(5b) I don't know what happened.

한편 앞서 설명하였듯이 '*believe, think*' 동사들의 경우 의문절이 목적절이 될 때 의문사는 전체 문장의 앞에 위치하게 된다.

(6a) Who likes this book?

(6b) Who do you believe likes this book? (NOT, Do you believe who likes this book?)

(7a) How did you select this article?

(7b) How do you believe I selected this article? (NOT, Do you believe how I selected this article?)

(8a) What can make you a good tennis player?

(8b) What do you think can make you a good tennis player? (NOT, Do you think what can make you a good tennis player?)

(9a) Where are you going?

(9b) Where do you think you're going? (NOT, Do you think where you're going?)

C-3. 명사절과 명사구

앞서 영어동사의 용례에서 살펴보았듯이 영어의 특정 동사들은 명사절이 아닌 '*to*-부정사'나 동명사 등의 명사구만을 목적어로 취한다. 또한 같은 동사가 명사절뿐만 아니라 명사구를 목적어로 취하기도 한다. 이 때 (1)~(4)의 문장들에서처럼 명사절과 '*to*-부정사'가 둘 다 동사의 목적어가 되는 경우는 의미의 차이를 보이기도 한다. (6)~(8)의 문장들은 해당 동사가 주어의 보어와 목적어의 보충어로 '*to*-부정사'의 명사구를 취하는 경우를 보여준다.

(1a) Someone told me that there are 20 people in a room. ('말하다'의 의미)

(1b) The doctor told me to stay in bed for a few days. ('지시/권고하다'의 의미)

(2a) I asked him if he would come up with a few options. ('묻다'의 의미)

(2b) Ann asked me not to tell anybody what happened. ('요청하다'의 의미)

(3a) I regret to inform you that you have failed the test. ('유감이다'의 의미)

(3b) I regret going to Europe. ('후회하다'의 의미)

(4a) I need to make drastic changes. (능동의 의미)

(4b) Their drainage and guttering needs fixing. (수동의 의미)

(5a) Would you mind if I ask you a few questions?

(5b) I don't mind doing it for the kids.

(6a) We expected to be late.

(6b) We expected Tom to be late.

(7a) Would you like to go now?

(7b) Would you like me to go now?

(8a) He doesn't want to know.

(8b) He doesn't want anybody to know.

D. 관계절(형용사절)

관계절(Relative Clause)은 명사 뒤에서 명사를 수식하는 형용사절을 말한다. 한국어에서는 형용사와 형용사절 모두 반드시 수식하는 명사의 앞에 위치하지만 영어의 경우 형용사는 명사의 앞에, 형용사구와 형용사절은 명사의 뒤에 온다. 따라서 영어의 명사는 앞에는 한정사와 형용사가, 뒤에는 형용사구와 형용사절이 수식하게 된다. 관계절은 일반적인 형용사절의 역할을 하는 한정적 용법과 추가 정보를 제공하는 기능을 하는 비한정적 용법으로 구분된다.

D-1. 관계절의 한정적 용법

관계절은 앞의 명사를 수식하는 형용사절이다. 즉 문장이 명사를 수식하게 되며 이 때 관계대명사가 앞의 명사 혹은 선행사를 뒤의 관계절(형용사절)과 연결시켜준다. 이렇게 형용사절의 기능을 하는 관계절을 한정적 관계절(Defining Relative Clause)이라고 한다. 이 때 앞에서 수식받는 명사(혹은 선행사)가 관계절 안에서 문법적 기능을 하기 때문에 관계대명사를 제외한 관계절 문장은 문법적 구성요소가 하나 빠진 비문법적인 문장이 된다. 관계절의 다양한 구성과 그 용례를 살펴보면 다음과 같다.

[1] 선행사(관계대명사)가 관계절 안의 주어의 역할을 하는 경우

아래의 문장 (1a)과 (1b)의 '*a man*'과 '*him(the man)*'은 동일한 사람을 가리키며 (1a) 문장이 (1b)의 '*him(the man)*'을 수식하는 관계절로 연결된 문장은 (1c)이다. (1c)에서 관계대명사 '*who*'가 가리키는 '*the man*'은 관계절의 주어의 역할을 하게 된다.

(1a) A man called you yesterday.

(1b) This morning I met with him(the man).

(1c) 오늘 아침 어제 너에게 전화했던 그 남자를 내가 만났다.

⇒ This morning I met with the man who Ø called you yesterday.

(2a) The little girl is playing the violin.

(2b) The girl is my cousin.

(2c) 바이올린을 연주하고 있는 저 어린 소녀는 내 사촌이다.

⇒ The little girl who Ø is playing the violin is my cousin.

관계대명사는 앞의 선행사가 사람일 경우 '*who*'를, 그렇지 않을 경우 '*which*'를 사용하게 된다. 다른 관계대명사인 '*that*'는 선행사가 주로 사물일 경우 사용되나 사람인 경우에 사용되기도 한다. 다음은 선행사가 관계절의 주어의 역할을 하는 다른 예들이다.

(3) I told you about the woman who lives next door.

(4) Students who can develop independent learning skills often achieve good academic results.

(5) Do you see the cat which is lying on the roof?

(6) There is a new book that investigates the controversy over political reforms in Hong Kong.

(7) Computer games that involve fighting and shooting apparently have a negative effect on young people.

[2] 선행사(관계대명사)가 관계절 안의 동사의 목적어의 역할을 하는 경우

아래 (8a) 문장의 목적어 '*the books*'는 (8b)의 문장에서 주어의 역할을 하는 '*these books*'와 동일한 것이다. (8a) 문장이 (8b)의 '*these books*'를 수식하는 관계절로 사용된 문장은 (8c)이다. 또한 (9a)의 '*uncle Boris*'와 (9b)의 '*him*'은 같은 사람이며 (9b) 문장이 관계절로 쓰인 복합절은 (9c)이다. 이 때 사람을 나타내는 선행사가 관계절의 목적어 역할을 할 경우는 원래 '*whom*'이 사용되었으나 지금은 '*who*'가 더 자주 쓰이며 드물게 'that'이 쓰이기도 한다. 선행사가 사람이 아닐 경우에는 '*which*'와 '*that*'이 쓰인다. 또한 관계절 안에서 목적어의 기능을 하는 경우, 주어의 기능을 하는 경우와 달리 관계대명사가 생략되기도 한다. (10a)의 '*the book*'과 (10b)의 '*the book*'은 공통된 대상이며 이 때 (10b)의 문장이 (10a)의 '*the book*'을 수식하는 경우 (10c)와 같은 복합절이 된다. (11)의 문장들의 경우 '*David Marchand*'와 '*him*'이 동일인물이며 (11b)가 (11a)의 '*David marchand*'를 수식하는 관계절은 (11c)에 제시되어 있다.

(8a) You see the books here.

(8b) These books are special.

(8c) 여기 네가 보는(네 앞에 있는) 이 책들은 특별한 책들이다.

⇒ These books (which/that) you see Ø here are special.

(9a) My uncle Boris is a writer.

(9b) You met him earlier today.

(9c) 어제 네가 만난 내 삼촌 Boris는 작가이다.

⇒ My uncle Boris (who/whom) you met Ø earlier today is a writer.

(10a) I have really enjoyed the book.

(10b) You gave me the book for my birthday.

(10c) 내 생일 선물로 네가 준 그 책 정말 재미있게 잘 읽었다.

⇒ I have really enjoyed the book (which/that) you gave me Ø for my birthday.

(11a) David Marchand has been assigned to my team.

(11b) I find him unbearable.

(11c) 내가 견디지 못할 정도로 싫어하는 David Marchand가 우리 팀에 배정되었다.

⇒ David Marchand (who/whom) I find Ø unbearable has been assigned to my team.

(12)~(17)의 문장들은 선행사가 관계절의 목적어의 역할을 하는 다른 예들이다.

(12) Can I borrow the CD (which/that) you bought?

(13) The boy (who/whom) we met yesterday is very nice.

(14) The designer (who/whom) you saw at the party last night is Giorgio Armani!

(15) The doctor (who/whom) I was hoping to see wasn't on duty.

(16) Many politicians have refused to disavow statements (which/that) experts have widely debunked as inaccurate.

(17) I would like to see the CNN interview of the five Cuban heroes (who/whom) they call 'terrorists'.

[3] 선행사(관계대명사)가 관계절 안의 전치사의 목적어의 역할을 하는 경우

때로는 관계절 안에서 전치사의 목적어가 선행사와 중복되는 경우가 있다. 이때는 선행사를 가리키는 관계대명사 앞에 전치사가 위치할 수 있다. 이런 경우 '*that*'이 관계대명사가 될 수 없고 관계대명사가 생략될 수 없으며 반드시 목적격으로 쓰여야 한다. 따라서 전치사가 관계절 앞에 위치하는 (18c) 문장에서는 전치사 뒤에 목적격 관계대명사 '*whom*'이 쓰인다. 그러나 (18d)처럼 전치사가 관계절 안에 남을 때는 관계대명사로 주격과 목적격이 쓰일 수 있으며 동사의 목적어로 쓰일 때처럼 관계대명사가 생략되기도 한다. 즉 전치사가 관계절의 앞에 위치하는 경우에는 '의미상 목적어임에도 관계절의 앞에 위치하면 목적격 대신 주격 관계대명사가 쓰일 수 있고 동시에 관계대명사가 생략될 수 있다'는 조건보다 '전치사 바로 뒤에는 목적어가 와야 하므로 목적격 관계대명사가 사용되어야 한다'는 조건이 더 우선적으로 적용된다.[1)]

(18a) This is a girl.
(18b) I spoke of her.
(18c) This is the girl of whom I spoke.
(18d) This is the girl (who/whom) I spoke of.
(19a) Tom belonged to the team.
(19b) The team won the game.
(19c) The team to which Tom belonged won the game.
(19d) The team (which) Tom belonged to won the game.

[4] 소유격 관계대명사의 예

아래의 예문 (20)의 경우 중복되는 부분은 (20a)의 'a man'과 (20b)의 'his'이다. 이를 관계절로 연결하면 (20c)가 된다. 즉 소유격 관계대명사 '*whose*'가 쓰인다. 소유격 관계대명사는 일반적으로 '*whose*'가 쓰이나 드물게 '*of which*'가 쓰이기도 한다.

1) 이는 의문절의 경우 의문사가 동사의 목적어로 쓰여도 주격의문사가 쓰이지만 전치사가 앞에 나올 때는 목적격 의문사가 쓰이는 현상과 유사하다.
To whom are you speaking? = Who are you speaking to?
For whom are you buying the present? = Who are you buying the present for?

(20a) On the street I saw a man.

(20b) His car was stolen.

(20c) On the street I saw a man whose car was stolen.

(21a) They live in a house.

(21b) Its roof is full of holes.

(21c) They live in the house whose roof is full of holes.

(22a) All students should immediately go to the library for a tour.

(22b) Their registration numbers begin with 374.

(22c) All students whose registration numbers begin with 374 should immediately go to the library for a tour.

(23a) The artist is coming to our area soon.

(23b) I adore his paintings.

(23c) The artist whose paintings I adore is coming to our area soon.

[5] 관계대명사 앞에 양이나 수를 한정하는 수식이 오는 경우

아래의 (24a)와 (24b) 문장은 '*three brothers*'와 '*them*'이 중복된다. 이 경우 (24b)가 (24a)를 수식하는 관계절일 경우 (24c)에서처럼 관계대명사 앞에 'two of'가 수식하게 되어 'two of whom'으로 쓰인다.

(24a) Mary has three brothers.

(24b) Two of them are married.

(24c) Mary has three brothers two of whom/*who are married.

(25a) My life has been full of terrible misfortunes.

(25b) Most of them never happened.

(25c) My life has been full of terrible misfortunes most of which never happened.

D-2. 관계절의 비한정적 용법

앞서 살펴본 관계절은 관계절이 선행사를 한정하는 형용사절에 해당되는 예들이다. 한정적 용법에서의 관계절은 선행사를 수식하는 역할을 하지만 비한정적 용법에서는 한정하기보다는 추가 정보를 제공한다. 이렇게 관계절이 추가 정보를 제공하는 용례로 사용될 때 이를 관계절의 비한정적 용법(Non-defining Relative Clause) 혹은 계속적 용법(Descriptive Relative Clause)이라고 한다. 관계절의 비한정적 용례는 다음과 같다.

[1] 앞의 선행사에 관해 추가 정보를 제시하는 경우

비한정적 용법에서는 관계절을 comma로 구분하며 이때 관계대명사 '*that*'은 사용되지 않는다. 또한 비한정적 용법의 관계대명사는 절대로 생략되지 않는다. 그리고 (7)~(12)의 문장에서 보듯이 관계대명사 앞에 수식어가 오는 관계절의 경우에는 특히 비한정적 용법으로 많이 쓰인다.

(1) I would like you to meet our auditor, who has worked here for three years.

(2) My students, who are all adults, are learning English to get a better job.

(3) The textbooks, which the students like, have lots of helpful examples.

(4) John F. Kennedy, <u>who was assassinated in 1963</u>, was the first Catholic president.

(5) The highest mountain in the world, <u>which is Mount Everest</u>, is located in Asia.

(6) The Empire State Building, <u>which many tourists visit each year</u>, is the second tallest building in New York.

(7) My students, <u>many of whom are from Europe</u>, are learning English to get a better job.

(8) The textbooks, <u>some of which the students like</u>, have helpful examples.

(9) Walt Disney was devoted to his children, <u>all of whom adored their father</u>.

(10) An explosion which injured four men, <u>two of whom are likely to die</u>, took place on the river front this morning at the freight-house entrance of the People's Line Steamboat Company.

(11) This book consists of eleven essays written by eight authors, <u>all of whom have had significant experience in telecommunications</u>.

(12) This left the Court with eight Republican-appointed justices, <u>five of whom had been appointed by Presidents Reagan or Bush</u>.

[2] 관계대명사 'which'가 앞의 문장을 지시하는 경우

비한정적 용법에서 앞의 문장 전체를 관계대명사가 가리킬 수 있으며 이때 관계대명사는 반드시 '*which*'가 쓰여야 한다. 가령 아래 (13a)와 (14a)에서 앞 문장 전체를 가리키는 대명사 '*that*'과 '*it*'의 기능을 (13b)와 (14b)의 관계절에서는 관계대명사 '*which*'가 하고 있다.

(13a) Sheila couldn't come to the party. That was a pity.

(13b) Sheila couldn't come to the party, which was a pity.

(14a) Taylor easily gives up. It always makes his mom worried.

(14b) Taylor easily gives up, which always makes his mom worried.

D-3. 관계부사절

한편 의미상 시간이나 장소, 이유 등을 나타내는 부사절이 선행사를 수식할 수도 있게 되는데 이때 앞의 선행사와 뒤의 문장을 연결하는 것이 관계부사(Relative Adverb)이다. 아래 (1a)의 문장의 '*Seoul*'이 (1b)의 문장에서 전치사와 함께 쓰여 장소를 나타낼 때 (1c)에서처럼 뒤에 부사절이 앞의 선행사 '*Seoul*'을 수식하게 되며 이때 관계부사 '*where*'가 쓰인다. 이때 가끔 '*that*'이 관계부사로 쓰이기도 한다. 관계대명사를 제외하고 불완전한 문장이 오는 관계절과 달리 관계부사절에서 관계부사를 제외한 관계절은 문법적인 문장을 구성한다. 관계부사절에도 한정과 비한정의 용법이 다 사용된다. 관계부사절의 예는 아래와 같다.

(1a) Mrs Kim likes Seoul.

(1b) Her daughter lives in Seoul.

(1c) Mrs Kim likes Seoul, where her daughter lives.

(2a) My friends are still talking about the day.

(2b) On that day I fell in the river.

(2c) My friends are still talking about the day when I fell in the river.

(3a) Tourists in New Orleans visit the Old Mint.

(3b) At that place United States currency used to be made.

(3c) Tourists in New Orleans visit the Old Mint where United States currency used to be made.

(4a) You have not given me any reason.

(4b) For which reason should I go out with you?

(4c) You have not given me any reason why I should go out with you.

관계부사절에서 관계부사 또는 앞의 선행사가 생략될 수 있으며 그 예들은 다음과 같다. (7)과 (8)의 예문에서 관계절은 선행사의 생략의 결과 궁극적으로 보어의 역할을 하는 명사절이 된다.

(5) This is the place (where) I was born.

(6) Now is the time (when) Frank must go.

(7) This is where the healing begins.

(8) This is why you are fat.

D-4. 선행사를 포함하는 관계대명사 'what'의 용법

선행사와 관계대명사가 혼합된 복합 관계대명사 '*what*'는 '*the thing(s) that*'의 의미를 갖는다. '*What*'은 뒤로는 관계절을 이끌지만 그 자체는 선행사를 포함하여 문장의 주어, 보어 및 목적어로 쓰이므로 명사절이 된다. '*What*'이 쓰인 문장의 예들은 다음과 같다.

(1) This is what I was trying to tell you.

(2) What he did is clearly impossible, but I saw him do it.

(3) What You See Is What You Get (WYSIWYG).

(4) I know what you did last summer.

(5) In the restaurant industry we have what's called(what we call) 'Truth in Menu.'

(6) The truth is things aren't always what they appear to be.

(7) Several thousand Egyptians protested Friday what they said was the government's systematic use of torture.

복합절 관련 연습문제

1. 다음의 문장 중 종속절인 부사절을 부사구로 만드시오.

(1) When we arrived at the mountain, we began to set up camp.

(2) After we had put on our hiking boots, we set off down the trail.

(3) Since he loves music so much, he decided to go to a conservatory.

(4) As I was a student, I was naturally interested in an effective way to solve the problem.

(5) Though I admit what you say, I still think you are wrong.

(6) When they are compared with last year, our earnings this year were up 23% despite the repeated rumors to the contrary.

(7) Since he was exhausted from a day's work, he went to bed earlier than usual.

(8) As he has been taught English since his childhood, he is a good speaker of English.

2. 다음의 문장을 주어진 동사를 이용하여 영작하시오. (명사절 만들기)

(1) 우리 언니 만나본 적 없지? *(think)*

(2) 그녀가 집에 없다고 생각해. *(believe)*

(3) 회의에 가지 못한 것을 후회했다. *(regret)*

(4) 멋진 시간 갖기를 바란다. *(hope)*

(5) 그는 내가 대통령을 만나야한다고 제안했다. *(suggest)*

(6) 그는 제주도에 가려면 비용이 얼마나 드는지 내게 물었다. *(ask)*

(7) 유감스럽게도 시험에 합격하지 못하신 것을 알려 드립니다. (시험에 합격하지 못하신 것을 알리게 되어서 유감스럽습니다.) *(regret to inform)*

(8) 그녀가 아직 전화를 안했다니 놀랍다. *(be surprised)*

(9) 그녀가 왜 나랑 데이트하고 싶어 하는 걸까? *(wonder)*

(10) 이것이 무엇을 의미하는지 내가 (너에게) 설명해 줄게. *(explain)*

(11) 그가 아직 침대에 누워 있다는 사실이 나를 놀라게 했다. *(surprise)*

(12) 그녀는 관심이 없다는 사실을 분명히 했다. *(make it clear)*

3. 다음의 문장을 영작하시오. (부사절 만들기)

(1) 퇴근하고 집에 오면 Ellen은 신문읽기를 좋아한다.

(2) 오늘 아침 직장에 가기 전에 나는 한 잔의 차를 마셨다.

(3) 비록 열심히 공부했지만 시험에 합격하지 못했다.

(4) 내일 추우면 집에 머무를 것이다.

(5) 학교를 졸업한 이래로(졸업해서부터) 그는 세 가지 직업을 갖았다.

(6) 우리가 이야기하는 동안 그는 계속해서 방해를 했다. (말이 끊기게 했다.)

(7) 날씨가 너무 추워서 그는 손가락에 감각이 없었다. (감각을 느낄 수 없었다.)

(8) 내가 만약 그의 번호를 안다면 전화할 텐데. (전화번호를 몰라서 전화하지 못한다.)

(9) 어제 밤 파티에 갔더라면 많은 사람들을 만났을 텐데. (가지 않아서 만나지 못했다.)

4. 다음의 문장을 영작하시오. (관계절/형용사절 만들기)

(1) 그는 무색의 희한한 눈을 가졌다.

⇒ He has hideous eyes________________________________.

a. He has hideous eyes.

b. These eyes are also colorless.

(2) Main Street에 줄지어 심어져 있는 나무들은 곧 베일 예정이다.

⇒ The trees ______________________________ are going to be cut down soon.

a. The trees are going to be cut down soon.

b. The trees line Main Street.

(3) 기차역 근처에 있는 Kennedy빌딩에서 여권을 발급받으실 수 있습니다.

⇒ You can get your passport renewed at the Kennedy building,

____.

a. You can get your passport renewed at the Kennedy building.

b. The Kennedy building is located near the train station.

(4) 여기서 수년을 공부하며 지낸 모든 화가들이 유명해지는 것은 아니다.

⇒ Not all artists ____

become famous.

a. Not all artists have spent years studying here.

b. Not all artists become famous.

(5) Jane이 근무하는 회사는 London에 본거지를 둔 회사이다.

⇒ The company ____ is based in London.

a. The company is based in London.

b. Jane works for the company.

(6) 친구들은 내가 강물에 빠졌던 그 날을 아직도 이야기 하고 있다.

⇒ My friends are still talking about the day____________________ ________________.

a. My friends are still talking about the day.

b. On that day I fell in the river.

(7) New Orleans에 가는 여행객들은 (그곳에서) 미국의 화폐가 만들어지던 the Old Mint를 방문한다.

⇒ Tourists in New Orleans visit the Old Mint __________________ ________________________.

a. Tourists in New Orleans visit the Old Mint.

b. At that place United States currency used to be made.

(8) 네가 사려던 그 집은 이미 팔려버렸다.

⇒ The house ____ has already been sold.

a. The house has already been sold.

b. You are thinking about buying the house.

(9) 나는 아무 말도 하지 않았고 그 사실이 그를 더욱 격분하게 만들었다.

⇒ I said nothing, ______________________________.

a. I said nothing.

b. That (the fact that I said nothing) made him more furious.

(10) Elliott이라는 이름을 가진 어린 소년의 친구인 E.T.(*Extra Terrestrial*, 영화의 주인공)는 선의 상징이다.

⇒ E.T. ______________________________ is the epitome of goodness.

a. E.T. is the epitome of goodness.

b. He is the friend of a young boy.

c. The boy is named Elliott.

5. 다음의 주어진 문장을 영작하시오.

(1) 내가 지금 신고 있는 신발은 편하지(*convenient*) 않다.

(2) 신입생들(*freshmen*)에게 주어진 그 과제(*assignment*)는 어렵다.

(3) 많은 단어들은 발음되지(*pronounce*) 않는 문자들을 포함한다.

(4) 많은 꽃들을 연구하는 연구원(*researchers*)들이 있었다.

(5) 내가 사고 싶었던 초콜릿은 파는 것(판매용)이 아니었다.

(6) 오늘 해야 할 일을 내일로 미루지(*postpone, put off*) 마라.

(7) 창문이(*its windows*)이 아주 큰 저 집이 마을에서 가장 오래 되었다.

(8) 그의 음악을 내가 사랑하는(*love, adore*) pianist가 다음 달 한국에 온다.

(9) 내가 야채를 자주 사던 그 작은 가게(*small store*)가 문을 닫고(*be closed*) 말았다.

E. 관계절과 형용사구

핵심어인 명사를 뒤에서 수식하는 것은 관계절 이외에 앞서 살펴 본 전치사구, '*to*'-부정사와 더불어 관계절에서 파생된 분사형(-ing/-ed) 형용사구가 있다. 특히 관계절에서 파생된 형용사구는 관계절을 간략하게 만드는 형용사구 구문으로서 자주 사용된다.

E-1. 관계절에서 파생된 형용사구 ('-ing/-ed' Participles)

형용사절인 관계절은 선행사가 관계절의 주어의 역할을 할 경우 분사형 형태로 쓰여 형용사구로 줄일 수 있다. 이 때 관계절 안의 동사가 자동사이거나 능동으로 쓰인 타동사이면 능동형 현재 분사형 '*-ing*'가 쓰이며 타동사가 수동태로 쓰였을 경우 수동태 과거분사형 '*-ed*'가 쓰여 형용사구를 형성한다. 아래의 예문들 중 (b)는 관계절을 분사 형태인 형용사구로 만든 문장들이다.

(1a) Police <u>that are investigating/that investigate the crime</u> are looking for three men.
(1b) Police <u>investigating the crime</u> are looking for three men.
(2a) Can you think of the name of a flower <u>that begins with 'T'</u>?
(2b) Can you think of the name of a flower <u>beginning with'T'</u>?
(3a) Some of the people <u>who are invited to the party</u> can't come.

(3b) Some of the people invited to the party can't come.

(4a) Most of the goods which are made in this factory are exported.

(4b) Most of the goods made in this factory are exported.

(5a) There were some children who were swimming in the river.

(5b) There were some children swimming in the river.

(6a) When they get classified information, they should go to the government agencies that are involved.

(6b) When they get classified information, they should go to the government agencies involved.

E-2. 분사 형태의 형용사

동사의 분사형은 또한 명사 앞에 위치하여 형용사로 쓰이기도 한다. 감정을 나타내는 타동사의 경우 의미에 따라 현재 분사형과 과거 분사형의 형태로 쓰여 명사를 수식하는 일반 형용사처럼 사용된다. 한편 아래 (7)의 예에서 보면 동사에서 파생되어 형용사로 쓰인 '*anticipated*'를 수식하는 부사가 형용사를 수식하는 데 일반적으로 사용되는 '*very*'가 아닌 '*much*'가 여전히 사용되고 있음을 알 수 있다.

(1) It's sometimes embarrassing when you have to ask people for money.

(2) Do you easily get embarrassed?

(3) She has really learned very fast. She has made astonishing progress.

(4) It was a really terrifying experience. Afterwards everybody was very shocked.

(5) Why do you always look so bored? Is your life really so boring?

(6) I would like to know about the areas of specialties in dentistry which are the least demanding as far as physical strength.

(7) Mr. Parker will deliver his much-anticipated speech this afternoon.

(8) This is a trying time for all of us.

E-3. 기타 : 복합 형용사와 비교 구문

한편 분사형을 이용하여 새롭게 복합 형용사를 만들 수 있으며 이러한 어법은 다양한 표현의 어휘를 생성해 낼 수 있는 효과적인 방식으로 자주 사용된다.

[1] 분사에서 파생된 복합 형용사

동사에 첨가되어 절을 구로 만드는 기능을 하는 분사형 어미 '*-ing*'와 '*-ed*'는 각각 의미에 따라 능동으로 쓰였을 경우 앞에 목적어가, 수동으로 쓰였을 경우 앞에 부사 등이 위치하여 복합 형용사로 쓰인다. 가령 '*time-consuming*'이란 표현은 '*something that consumes time*'이라는 절에서 파생된 것이다. 이렇듯 영어에서는 분사형 '*-ing*'와 '*-ed*'를 이용하여 동사를 형용사로 만든 후 그 동사의 목적어나 다른 수식어에 해당되는 것을 앞에 위치하여 복합어를 생성한다. 이는 앞에서 언급한 문장부사와 함께 현대영어에서 자주 이용되는 조어법이기도 하다.

(1) 과거분사 '-ed'를 이용한 경우

loud-mouthed hooligans; a middle-aged lady; rose-tinted glasses; a red-cheeked girl; a pig-headed man; a level-headed person; a home–grown pig; an over–rated actor; a cold–blooded murderer; an old–fashioned house; brightly–lit streets; sun–dried tomatoes; a God–given talent; Disney's saccharin coated kiddie flicks; a Korea–born skater; US–made cars; Hardboiled crime fiction; a well–educated person; a clearcut case; a spellbound audience, financially hard–pressed, food–borne disease, farm raised cattle, etc.

(2) 현재분사 '–ing'을 이용한 경우

an awe–inspiring personality; a long–lasting affair; a far–reaching decision; a late–blooming actress; a time–consuming job; a mind–boggling thing; a gorgeous–looking girl; a good–looking chef; free–standing cooker; labour–saving devices; a never–ending story; an eye–popping experience; a far–fetching speculation; a crowd–pleasing performance; a heart–warming story; a hard–working man; a soul–searching process; an eye–catching site; a breathtaking view; a hard–hitting report; spellbinding characters, etc.

[2] 비교 구문

보통 '*more~than*', '*as~as~*'와 같은 비교 구문은 두 가지를 비교하는 문장이다 보니 관계절과 마찬가지로 중복되는 부분은 생략하게 된다. 따라서 아래의 예문들에서 보듯이 '*as*'나 '*than*' 뒤에는 불완전한 문장이 나오게 된다.

(1) He is as great a scholar as ever lived.
(2) There have been four times as many salmonella outbreaks detected as would normally be expected.

(3) This phenomenon is not as outrageous as it seems.

(4) She gave him more sympathy than I gave him.

(5) There is more demand for fish than the sea alone can provide.

(6) He was more upset than I was.

분사형과 관련한 연습문제

1. 다음의 밑줄 친 관계절을 분사형을 이용하여 형용사구로 만드시오.

(1) Police who are investigating the crime are looking for three men.

(2) Can you think of the name of a flower that begins with 'T'?

(3) A few days after the interview, I received a letter that offered me the job.

(4-5) Companies which offers products that are related to DNA technology are invited to display their products at the meeting.

(6) Chain reactions which involve the fast neutrons can be controlled in a reactor.

(7) Human eyes are remarkable optical instruments which consist of very specialized structures.

(8) The people who appeared in his paintings were mostly farmers and laborers.

(10) The reporters who were assigned to South Africa could not go there due to the terror.

(11) Manet's paintings that shocked the French people most was 'Lumcheon in the Grass.'

(12) Anna Robertson Moses who was also known as Grandma

Moses is considered the Grande Dame of U.S. art.

(13) Grandma Moses who painted without any formal training remains one of the twentieth century's most famous primitive artists.

(14) These colorful pictures which are called 'primitive' are based on her early life in rural New York.

2. (   ) 안에 밑줄 친 동사를 주어진 의미에 맞게 '–ing'나 '–ed'의 분사형으로 변형하여 형용사로 만들어 적으시오.

(1) My history teacher always talks in a monotone and never looks at the students. He is the most (bore(지루한):   ) teacher I have.

(2) Veronica has just gotten a job with an architect's firm. She is doing an excellent job. Her employer is (surprise(놀라다) :   ).

(3–6) I didn't understand the (confuse(혼동되는) :   ) tax forms that I got from the government. I was so (worry(걱정되다) :   ) about them that I asked my neighbor to help me. However, he gave me a lot of (mislead(잘못된) :   ) information. Finally I went the tax consultant who had a (depress(어두운, 침울한) :   ) office. He helped me to fill out the forms correctly.

(7) Mr. Lee was a very (dedicate(헌신적인) :   ) member of the team because he always had good ideas and was willing to sacrifice himself.

(8) Engineering is one of the most time–consuming and (demand(힘든, 노력을 필요로 하는) :   ) programs in university.

(9) Are you going to keep me (wait(기다리는) :   ) all day long?

(10) Star Wars III is arguably the most (anticipate(기대되는) :   ) movie of all time.

IV

전치사의 활용

IV 전치사의 활용

영어에서 전치사(Preposition)는 명사 앞에 쓰여 그 명사와 함께 소유, 위치, 시간, 방향, 이유, 상태, 양보 등의 다양한 의미를 표현한다. 따라서 전치사는 일반적으로 뒤의 명사와 함께 문장 안에서 앞의 명사를 수식하는 형용사구나 문장에 부가적 의미를 부여하는 부사구의 역할을 한다. 그러나 이러한 일반적인 전치사의 용례 이외에도 전치사의 활용은 다음과 같이 다양하다. 첫째, 동사의 뒤에 첨가되어 [동사 + 전치사]의 구동사(Phrasal Verb)를 형성함으로써 다양한 표현이 파생되거나 자동사가 타동사처럼 활용될 수 있도록 한다. 둘째, 'be-동사'와 형용사 뒤에 쓰여 [be + 형용사 + 전치사] 구문이 일종의 구동사의 기능을 하게 만든다. 셋째, 동사에서 파생된 명사나 일반 명사의 뒤에 와서 그 명사의 의미를 보완하고 원래 절에서 동사로 쓰였을 때의 구문의 특징을 유지시키는 역할도 한다. 따라서 영어작문에 있어서 전치사의 다양한 용례를 학습하고 활용하는 것은 필수적이다.

A. 부사구를 구성하는 전치사

영어의 전치사들 중에서 위치, 시간, 방향 등을 표시할 때 자주 쓰이는 전치사들인 '*at, in, on, to*' 등의 용례는 다음과 같다.

A-1. 'AT'

'*At*'은 장소 또는 위치를 나타내며 보통 (1)과 (2)의 예들처럼 '*…에*'의 의미로 그 장소 안에 들어가거나 위에 있거나 하는 구체적 위치가 아닌 '*그 장소에 있다*'라는 의미로 쓰일 때 사용된다. 때로는 (3)의 문장에서처럼 어떤 위치의 구체적인 주소를 언급할 때 '*at*'이 쓰이며 (4)와 (5)의 예들처럼 큰 위치 안의 작은 위치를 의미할 때도 사용된다. (6)~(11)의 예들에서는 어느 장소나 모임에 출석해 있음을 뜻한다. 한편 (12)~(24)의 문장에서는 '*at*'이 구체적인 시각이나 '*지금, 당장, 밤에, 낮에, 한번에*' 등의 시간을 나타낼 때 사용되었다.

[1] 장소와 위치 용례

(1) The women are at the supermarket.
(2) I saw her at the parking lot.
(3) She lives at 3757, North, 52nd Street.
(4) He was waiting in the room at the door.
(5) He likes to sit in her apartment at the window facing the park.
(6) The children are at school.
(7) We aren't allowed to watch television when we are at dinner.
(8) They are at the movies.
(9) She is at a meeting.
(10) We discussed that topic at length at our meeting.
(11) You must not bother him; he is at work.

[2] 시간, 기관과 관련된 용례

(12) We are leaving at four thirty.
(13) They went home at midnight.

(14) We always eat lunch at noon.

(15) At first we thought this hike would be easy.

(16) I always read or study at night.

(17) We must pack up and leave at once.

(18) At present they are sleeping.

(19) After that long drive, we are home at last.

(20) At the beginning we tried to go too fast.

(21) At the end of the story, everybody was happy.

(22) I am very busy at the moment.

(23) The tall boy liked to go up the steps two or three at a time.

(24) Try to learn one step at a time, rather than three or four at once.

A-2. 'IN'

(1)~(3)의 예들에서 보듯이 '*in*'은 '*city, continent, country, state, town*' 등 규모가 큰 장소를 말할 때 사용된다. 혹은 (4)~(7)에서처럼 어느 장소나 위치의 안에 있는 것 또는 공간이 작은 무언가에 타는 것을 의미할 때 사용한다. 또한 (8)~(10)의 문장에서는 어느 장소에 머물러 있는 상태이거나 어느 단체나 그룹의 소속임을 의미한다. 시간과 관련해서는 '*at*'에 비해 비교적 범위가 넓은 편에 속한다. 한편 (17)과 (18)의 문장에서는 '*얼마의 시간이 지나서*'의 의미로 쓰인다. (19)~(23)에서는 '*…안으로, …쪽으로*'의 의미로 방향을 나타내며 (24)와 (25) 문장에서는 출처를 뜻하는 '*…에서*'의 의미로 쓰인다.

[1] 장소와 위치 용례

(1) We live in that house.

(2) He is staying in Europe.

(3) He lives in Seattle, Washington, in the U.S.A.

(4) He sat down in the chair and read his novel.

(5) The pencils are in the box.

(6) She is in her office, in that building, in room 302, in the corner.

(7) We were in the car, but they were in a helicopter.

(8) He can't come to the phone because he's in bed.

(9) There are seven people in our family.

(10) Your brother is the expert in that office.

[2] 시간, 기간과 관련된 용례

(11) She was born in the 1800s.

(12) He took his vacation in March.

(13) I work in the morning.

(14) My boss works in the afternoon.

(15) We relax in the evening.

(16) We lived there in the past, and we will live here in the future.

(17) She will be here in five minutes.

(18) He will be here in no time.

[3] 방향, 출처와 관련된 용례

(19) They went in the store.

(20) The girls came in this direction, and the boys went in the opposite direction.

(21) Please pour the juice in the glass.

(22) Bring him in!

(23) He didn't say that in his speech.

(24) I read it in the newspaper.

A-3. 'ON'

'*On*'은 '무언가 접촉하는 표면 위에서' 혹은 '*…의 표면에 인접한*'의 의미로 쓰인다. 한편 (13)~(16)의 예에서는 '*…의 표면 위로*'의 동작의 의미로 쓰인다. (17)~(20)의 문장에서는 공간이 비교적 넓은 탈것에 올라타거나 '*…을 타고*'의 의미로 쓰인다. 또한 날짜와 요일을 의미할 때 사용되며 (26)의 예에서처럼 '*시간에 딱 맞추어서*'의 의미로도 쓰인다.

[1] 접촉의 의미

(1) The newspaper is on the table.

(2) Please sign your name on the dotted line.

(3) He was standing on the corner of First Street and Maple Avenue.

(4) Let's have a barbecue on the balcony.

(5) She rides her bicycle on the sidewalk.

(6) There is a fly on the ceiling.

(7) The child pasted the picture on the page.

(8) That is the only place on earth where she feels safe.

(9) The porch is on the side of the house.

(10) What street is your house on?

(11) Their house is on the beach.

(12) He wrote it on paper.

(13) It rained on your bicycle last night.

(14) She jumped on the bed.

(15) She poured water on the plant.

(16) He sprinkled salt on the meat.

(17) She goes to work on the bus.

(18) They went on the train to Philadelphia.

(19) He came over on his bike.

(20) She was sore from riding on a horse.

[2] 날짜, 요일과 같은 특정한 시간을 나타낼 경우

(21) Congratulations on your graduation.

(22) They went out to dinner on their anniversary.

(23) They are leaving on Saturday (or any day).

(24) We are leaving on the ninth of August (or any date).

(25) They are going to New York on the weekend.

(26) Mary is always on time for class.

지금까지 살펴 본 부사적 용례의 '*in, at, on*' 전치사들의 활용을 비교해 보면 다음과 같다.

Preposition	Time	Place
In	Year, Month '*In 1999, In December*'	Country, State, City '*In Korea, In Utah, In London*'
On	Day, Date '*On Friday, On October 1*'	Street '*On Main Street, On 1st St.*'
At	Time '*At 9:00, At 11:30*'	Address '*At 254 West Main Street*'

A-4. 'TO'

'*TO*'는 '…로'의 의미로 쓰여 방향을 나타낸다. 또한 (7)~(11)의 예문에서는 '*…한테, …에게*'의 의미로 쓰이며 (12)~(14)의 예에서는 '*from… to…*'가 쓰여 '*…부터 …까지*'의 의미로 사용된다. 한편 '*to*'는 (15)~(18)의 예에서 보듯이 시간의 경과 혹은 '*…시 …분 전*' 등의 의미를 나타낸다.

[1] 방향이나 대상과 관련된 용례

(1) I'm going to bed.

(2) They ride to school on the bus.

(3) We go to the park every afternoon.

(4) Call when you get to the office.

(5) We wanted to go on a cruise to the Caribbean.

(6) He delivers the mail to the office.

(7) She mentioned her plans to me.

(8) He is a credit to his mother and father.

(9) The airplane noise is a disturbance to the neighborhood.

(10) He was very cruel to me.

(11) She has been hostile to her neighbors.

(12) We went from door to door with our information sheets.

(13) The bus rocked from side to side.

(14) They have door-to-door service. (from door to door)

[2] 시간의 용례

(15) They work from morning to night.

(16) He was here from two to five.

(17) It is ten (minutes) to three in the afternoon. (3시까지 10분, 즉 3시 10분 전)

(18) It was a quarter (fifteen minutes) to four.

B. 동사, 형용사, 명사와 함께 쓰이는 전치사

영어에서 전치사는 앞서 제시된 부사적 용례 이외에도 다양하게 쓰여 의미를 풍부하게 한다. 즉 동사, 형용사, 그리고 명사 뒤에 광범위하게 쓰여 보다 자연스럽고 세분화된 의미 표현을 가능하게 하고 문법 기능을 바꿔 자동사를 타동사로 쓸 수 있게 하기도 한다. 특히 명사나 형용사 뒤에 쓰이는 전치사는 원래 동사에서 같이 쓰이던 전치사가 해당 동사가 명사 혹은 형용사로 파생되었을 경우에 여전히 동일하게 쓰이는 경우가 많다. 전치사와의 조합이 만들어내는 다양한 표현은 다음과 같다.

B-1. 동사와 함께 쓰이는 전치사

전치사는 특히 동사와 자주 같이 쓰이는데 이럴 때 사용되는 전치사를 일반 전치사와 구문하여 불변화사라고 하며 이러한 [동사 + 불변화사] 구문을 구동사라고 한다. 전치사 혹은 불변화사는 때로는 자동사와 함께 쓰여 뒤에 오는 명사를 목적어로 취함으로써 본래의 자동사를 타동사로써 기능할 수 있도록 해주기도 한다. 구동사표현은 일반적으로 다양하고 자연스러운 묘사를 하는 데 사용된다. 동사와 전치사 조합은 아래의 몇몇 예를 비롯하여 그 용례가 무궁무진하다. 또한 구동사는 [동사 + 부사]의 조합을 이루기도 한다. 특히 구동사와 관련하여 주목해야 할 점은 (8d)의 예처럼 전치사 뒤에 종종 명사가 아닌 명사절이 목적어로 오기도 한다는 것이다. 이는 영어화자들이 동사와 불변화사의 조합인 구동사를 일종의 타동사로서 간주하기 때문인 것으로 추정할 수 있다.

(1a) I had to apologize for Frank.

(1b) I had to apologize to the hostess.

(1c) I apologized to Bridget for the misunderstanding.

(1d) I apologized for Frank to the hostess.

(1e) He was never able to apologize to himself for his past errors.

(2a) The child asked for a glass of water.

(2b) The diners asked the waiter for a type of wine the restaurant didn't have.

(2c) Janet asked us to a party Friday evening. Janet asked us for dinner.

(2d) Janet asked us to a party for dinner Friday evening.

(3a) Why did you have to bring that up? Why did you bring up

Walter? I hate talking about him!

(3b) We brought up the puppies carefully and sold them for a good profit.

(4a) I care for you too, Alice.

(4b) Will you care for my cat while I am away?

(5) This desk belongs to the company. You can't take it home!

(6) We had to give the money we found up to the police. We gave up the money to the police.

(7) All the children have grown up and the parents are left with a lot of debts.

(8a) I am looking for Mr. William Wilson. Do you know where he lives?

(8b) A baby-sitter is somebody who looks after other people's children.

(8c) Look at these flowers. Aren't they pretty?

(8d) Let us look at how these decisions will be considered and taken.

(9a) I searched for Ted everywhere, but he was already gone.

(9b) The police searched the suspect for hidden weapons.

(9c) Everyone searched the house for little Wally, but he was not to be found.

(10a) Whenever I think about him, I get goose bumps.

(10b) I think of you whenever I go to the restaurant where we used to eat.

(11) We hope for good weather on Friday.

(12) You know that you can rely/depend on me if you ever need

any help.

(13) What happened to Martha?

(14) They can't find work, so they beg for food.

(15a) Thank you for the invitation to your party next week.

(15b) I thanked everybody for all the help they had given me.

(16) The woman sitting opposite me on the train kept staring at me.

(17) We waited for Jim for half an hour but he never come.

(18) Please listen to me! I've got something important to tell you.

(19) Please don't shout at me! Be nice to me!

(20) Diane left Boston for Paris when she was 19.

(21) I love this music. It reminds me of a warm day in spring.

(22) Our neighbors complained to us about the noise we made last night.

(23a) She's not a well-known singer. Not many people have heard of her.

(23b) Did you hear about the accident last night?

(24) I don't really want to go out with Ian tonight. I'll have to think of an excuse.

(25) I congratulated her on winning the tournament.

(26) A football team consists of 11 players.

(27) You always blame me for everything.

(28) When you went to the theater with Paul, who paid for the tickets?

(29) It's not very pleasant when you are accused of something you didn't do.

(30) Sally is often not well. She suffers from very bad headaches.

(31) Jill provided me with all the information I needed.

(32) Steve gave me an empty bucket and told me to fill it with water.

(33) It wasn't easy but in the end we succeeded in finding a solution to the problem.

(34) Don't try and do two things together. Concentrate on one thing at a time.

(35) Jim is a photographer. He specializes/majors in sports photography.

(36) I prefer travelling by train to driving. It's much more pleasant.

(37) Somebody broke into my car and stole the radio.

(38) I felt quite cold but Peter insisted on having the window open.

(39) I spend quite a lot of money on books.

(40) Are you looking forward to the party next week?

(41) There was a bank robbery last week. The robbers got away with $500,000.

(42) The story she told you wasn't true. She made it up.

(43) Don't throw away that box. I want to keep it.

(44) We can turn the TV off. Nobody is watching it. (turn on vs turn off)

(45) I tried a jacket on in the shop but I didn't buy it.

(46) Please put your cigarette out. This is a no-smoking area.

(47) He contributed his ideas to the discussion.

(48) Patricia applied for admission to the university.

(49) Trucks are prohibited (kept/barred/stopped) from using residential streets.

(50) The farmers are hoping for rain.

(51) We will fight for our rights. We will fight against the enemy.

(52) May I help you with your luggage? That is very kind of you.

(53) I'm sorry I haven't written to you for so long. The reason for this is that I've been ill.

(54) His strange behaviors freaks people out.

한편 동사가 수동태가 되어 'be + -ed형'으로 전치사와 함께 자주 쓰인다. 이와 관련된 몇몇 예들은 다음과 같다.

(55) Max is known for his honesty.

(56) We always have the same food every day. I'm fed up with it.

(57) We enjoyed our holiday, but we were a bit disappointed with the hotel.

(58) Did you know that Liz is engaged/married to a friend of mine?

(59) Mack was tired of hearing about their trip to India.

(60) They were not satisfied with the result.

(61) He is accused of terrorism.

(62) His heart was filled with pride at that time.

(63) The committee is composed mainly of lawyers.

(64) She is dedicated to her job.

B-2. 형용사와 함께 쓰이는 전치사

전치사는 또한 '*be*-동사'나 불완전 자동사와 형용사 뒤에 쓰여 [be/자동사 + 형용사 + 전치사] 전체구문이 동사처럼 기능을 하게 된다. 그 예들은 다음과 같다.

(1) I needed money and Ian gave me some. That was generous of him.

(2a) May I help you with your luggage? That is very kind of you.

(2b) He has been very kind to me.

(3a) I wouldn't like to be in her position. I feel sorry for her.

(3b) I'm sorry about the smell of paint in this room. I've just decorated it.

(4) Why are you always so rude to your parents?

(5a) Can't you be nice to them?

(5b) It was very nice of you to do my shopping for me. Thank you very much.

(6) I can't understand people who are cruel to animals.

(7) Your camera is similar to mine but it isn't exactly the same.

(8) Mrs. Davis is a very keen gardener. She's very proud of her garden and loves showing it to visitors.

(9) My home town is not especially interesting. It's not famous for anything.

(10) I bet everyone here became aware of the dangers of smoking.

(11) Paul's comments were not relevant to the topic under discussion.

(12) We've got plenty to eat. The refrigerator is full of food.

(13) She is a very honest person. I don't think she is capable of telling a lie.

(14) John has no money of his own. He's totally dependent on his parents. (〈 *depend on*)

(15) I'm not very good at math.

(16) I am not familiar with that author's works.

B-3. 명사와 함께 쓰이는 전치사

명사의 경우도 자주 전치사가 함께 쓰인다. 특히 동사에서 파생된 명사의 경우 문장에서 동사로 쓰일 때는 주어나 목적어였던 다른 명사가 파생된 명사와 함께 쓰이면서 문법적으로 전치사가 필요하게 된다. 또한 전치사와 결합함으로써 보다 구체적이고 다양한 의미를 표현할 수 있게 된다. 이때 일반적으로 원래 동사이었을 때 함께 쓰이던 전치사를 그대로 사용하는 경향이 있다. 또한 유사한 의미군에 속한 명사들은 같은 전치사를 사용하는 경향이 있다. (괄호 안의 예들은 동사였을 때의 표현을 의미한다.)

(1a) We're trying to find a solution to the problem. (〈 *solve the problem*)

(1b) What was Emma's reaction to the news? *(〈 react to the news)*

(1c) I can't think of an answer to your question. *(〈 answer your question)*

(1d) I wrote to Jim last week, but I still haven't received a reply to my letter. *(〈 reply my letter)*

(1e) It wasn't a bad accident. The damage to the car wasn't serious. *(〈 damage the car)*

(2a) Sue has a good relationship with her brother. *(〈 relate with)*

(2b) Since she left home two years ago, she had had little contact with her family. *(〈 contact her family)*

(2c) What is the difference between your job and mine?

(2d) The two companies are completely independent. There is no connection between them.

(3a) There has been a big increase in prices. *(〈 increase in prices)*

(3b) There has been a sharp rise in the cost of living in the past few years. *(〈 rise in the cost)*

(4a) I don't think there is any need for a new road. *(〈 need a new road)*

(4b) Carol has decided to give up her job. I don't know her reason for doing this.

(4c) The company has rejected the workers' demands for a rise in pay. *(〈 demand a rise in pay)*

C. 전치사 'of'

전치사 '*of*'는 [A of B]의 형태로 '*of B*'가 앞의 명사 A를 수식하는 형용사구로 자주 쓰인다. 이때 일반적으로 앞의 명사는 핵심어이며 뒤의 'A *of B*'는 그 핵심어를 수식하는 수식어인 형용사구이다. 이 경우 '*of*'는 속격(Genitive)의 의미로 쓰인다. 그러나 '*of*'가 늘 속격으로 쓰이는 것은 아니다. 가령 '*one of them*' 같은 예에서는 '*among*'의 의미로도 쓰이며 그 외에도 전치사 '*of*'는 목적격과 주격의 의미를 갖기도 한다. 이는 [A of B]의 구문 중 A에 파생명사가 올 경우 그 파생명사가 파생 이전의 동사로 쓰였을 때의 특징을 일부 보유하고 있기 때문이다. 즉 원래 동사가 타동사였을 경우 파생명사와 뒤에 따라 나오는 명사(원래 목적어)를 이어주는 '*of*'는 목적격의 의미를 갖으며 자동사였을 경우는 '*of*' 뒤의 명사가 원래 문장에서 주어였으므로 주격의 의미를 갖게 된다. 아래의 예에서 (4)의 '*return*'은 '*to return books*'의 의미에서 초래하여 전치사 'of'가 목적격의 관계로 쓰였지만 (5)에서는 '*The Economist returns*'의 자동사에서 초래하여 주격의 관계를 보여준다. 아래의 다른 예들 중 (6), (8)과 (9)에서는 'of'가 목적격으로 (7)과 (10)에서는 주격의 의미로 사용되고 있다.

(1) Returning of books should be made at the Self-Checking Machine or at Circulation Counter. (〈…*return books*)

(2) Keynes : The Rise, Fall, and Return of the 20th Century's Most Influential Economist (〈 *The 20th Century's Most Influential Economist rose, fell and returned*)

(3) Globalization of food production (〈 …*globalize food production*)

(4) Coming of age (〈 *Age comes*)

(5) Secure destruction of personal information (〈 …*securely destroy personal information*)

(6) Removal of skin tags. (〈 …*remove skin tags*)

(7) The arrival of Swine Flu (〈 *Swine Flu arrives*)

전치사 관련 연습문제

1. 적절한 전치사를 활용하여 주어진 문장을 영작하시오.

(1) 그를 정오에 만날 계획이다.

( ).

(2) 그는 LA에서 산다.

( ).

(3) 나는 차(*my car*)에 타서 집으로 향했다.

( ).

(4) 그 소설의 작가가 막 도착했다.

( ).

(5) 기차는 오후 12:30에 도착할 예정(*be due*)이다.

( ).

(6) 일요일에 나는 Paris로 떠날 것이다/떠날 예정이다.

( ).

(7) 내 여자 친구는 호텔에서 receptionist로 일한다.

( ).

(8) 그는 택시에서 내렸다.

( ).

(9) 우리는 버스에 올라탔다.

( ).

(10) 그는 2002년 5월 25일에 브라질에서 태어났다.

( ).

2. 적절한 전치사를 활용하여 주어진 표현을 영어로 바꾸시오.

(1) 회의에의 초대

(an invitation)

(2) 외국인 노동자들에의 의존

(the dependence)

(3) 성공에의 열쇠

(a key)

(4) 무릎을 꿇고

(knees)

(5) 그의 물리학에의 공헌(*contribution*)

(his contribution)

(6) 사람들의 무기에의 접근

(people's access)

(7) 법집행(*law enforcement*)을 지지하는 자들

(advocates)

(8) Parkinson's병을 갖고 있는 환자들

( )

(9) 우리의 고객 요구(*the needs of the customer*)에의 집중(*focus*)

( )

(10) Obama대통령은 연정(*coalition*)을 촉구(*call*…)해왔다.

( ).

(11) 이것을 그 큰 상자 안에 넣으시오.

( ).

(12) 그는 백혈병(*leukemia*)으로 30살의 나이에 죽었다.

( ).

(13) 나는 뮤지컬 가수가 되는 것을 꿈꾸어 왔다.

( ).

(14) 그들은 범인(*criminal, suspect*)을 잡기 위해서 학교를 뒤졌다(*search*).

( ).

(15) 우리 아이를 돌보아 주셔서 감사드립니다(*thank*).

( ).

(16) 저희들을 도와주시다니 정말 친절하십니다. (*It is*… 구문을 사용할 것.)

( ).

(17) 그는 회사의 파산(*bankruptcy*)에 대해 책임이(*responsible*) 없다고 주장했다(*argue that*…).

( ).

(18) 난 그의 천재성(*his genius*)에 대해 잘 알고(*aware*) 있어.

( ).

(19) 내가 말할 때는 좀 귀담아 들어라(*listen*).

( ).

(20) 앵커리지(*Anchorage*)행 비행기(*flight*)편이 결항(*cancel*)되었습니다. 결항(*flight cancellation*)으로 인해 불편(*inconvenience*)을 끼치게 되어(*cause*) 승객여러분(*passengers*)께 사과드립니다(*apologize*).

( ).

Verb Index (동사 색인)

문법용어 색인

대학영작문 영어문장의 이해와 활용

초판 1쇄 발행 / 2016년 12월 9일
초판 2쇄 발행 / 2020년 3월 30일

저자 김종실
발행처 형설출판사
경기도 파주시 회동길 37-23 · 전화 (031) 955-2361~4 · 팩시밀리 (031) 955-2341
발행인 장진혁
등록 라-제9호 · 1962년 5월 1일
홈페이지 http://www.hyungseul.co.kr
e-mail hs@hyungseul.co.kr

정가 19,000원

ISBN 978-89-472-8118-8 93740

이 도서의 국립중앙도서관 출판시도서목록(CIP)은 서지정보유통지원시스템 홈페이지(http://seoji.nl.go.kr)와 국가자료공동목록시스템(http://www.nl.go.kr/kolisnet)에서 이용하실 수 있습니다.(CIP제어번호 : CIP2016021979)

대학영작문

영어문장의 이해와 활용